GCSE RELIGIOUS STUDIES

A STUDY OF THE GOSPEL OF MATTHEW

Juliana Gilbride

Colourpoint Educational

Rewarding Learning

ISBN: 978 1 906578 34 3

First Edition
First Impression

Layout and design: Colourpoint Books
Printed by: W&G Baird Ltd, Antrim

The Author

Juliana Gilbride, B.Ed (Hons), M.Ed, was part of a team of teachers who revised the Religious Studies GCSE Specification for CCEA (for first teaching in 2009). She is a Revisor for GCSE Religious Studies for CCEA, and has fifteen years experience of teaching Religious Studies in Northern Ireland.

Colourpoint
Educational

Colourpoint Books
Colourpoint House
Jubilee Business Park
21 Jubilee Road
Newtownards
County Down
Northern Ireland
BT23 4YH

Tel: 028 9182 6339
Fax: 028 9182 1900
E-mail: info@colourpoint.co.uk
Web site: www.colourpoint.co.uk

Acknowledgements

The ackowledgements on page 70 constitute an extension of this copyright page.

CONTENTS

For your folder In a Group Further Thinking

Chapter 1

BACKGROUND TO MATTHEW'S GOSPEL

The word 'Gospel' means 'good news'. It is comes from the Anglo-Saxon *god spel*, which can mean 'spell it out', 'speak out' or 'proclaim'. In the Bible the Gospels proclaim the good news about Jesus. There are four Gospels with four different writers: Matthew, Mark, Luke and John.

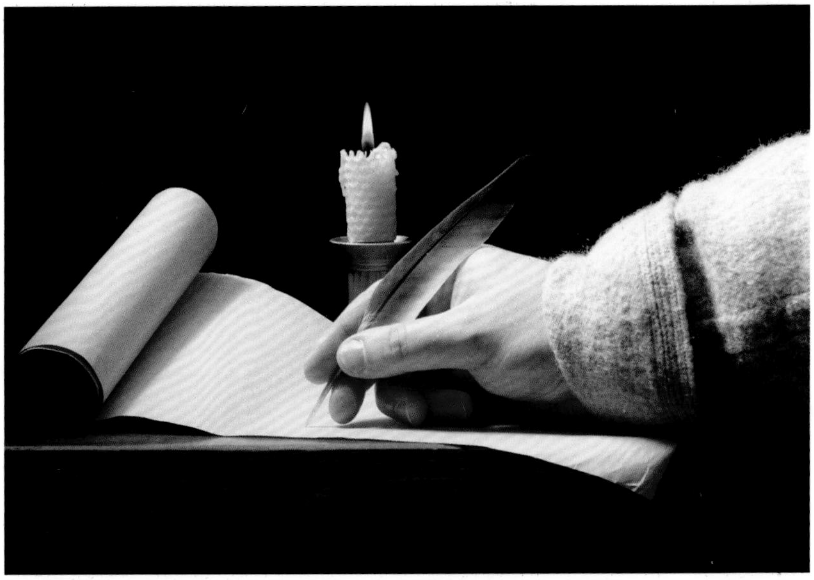

Each records the events of Jesus' life, death and resurrection. Three of the Gospels – Matthew, Mark and Luke – are very similar in content and structure. These are called the 'Synoptic Gospels'. The word *synoptic* means 'shared view'. Many passages from these three Gospels can be placed side by side to show how similar they are. For example, the story of Jesus' baptism and temptations (Matthew 3:13–4:11, Mark 1:9-13, Luke 3:19-4:19). The fourth account of Jesus' life, John's Gospel, is very different in style and content to the other three.

After Jesus' death, resurrection and ascension, many stories circulated about him. His disciples and close friends would have recalled incidents that other people would know nothing of. Each group of people would probably have remembered different events. At first these stories about Jesus were passed around by word of mouth. This is known as the '**Christian Oral Tradition**'.

Many of the early Christians believed that Jesus would return during their lifetime (the idea that Jesus will return is called the 'second coming' or *parousia.*) However, as time passed, those first Christians who had met Jesus began to die out. It was important that the stories about Jesus were preserved, so they were written down.

Besides the four Gospels included in the New Testament, there are a number of other documents that claim to give written accounts of Jesus' life. These other accounts have not been accepted by the church and are considered unreliable. Often they are written far too long after the event to be trusted.

The Gospel writers are called 'evangelists', that is, those who spread the good news about Jesus. Each writer tells the story of Jesus' life and death in their own unique way.

It would be too simple to describe the Gospels as 'biographies' of Jesus. You won't find many details on what Jesus looked like or what he did when he was growing up. Instead, the Gospel writers focused on the things that were important to them.

FACTS ABOUT THE GOSPELS

No one is certain when the Gospels first emerged. You might assume that Matthew's Gospel is the earliest book in the New Testament, because it comes first. However, if you look at the **timeline** you will realise that Paul's letters, such as Romans and Corinthians, seem to be the earliest books. Most scholars argue that Mark's Gospel, the shortest one, was the first to appear (around AD 64–65).

63 BC	Romans take over Palestine
4 BC 5 BC	Mary gives birth to Jesus
AD 25	Jesus begins his public ministry of preaching and healing
AD 28	Jesus is crucified by Pontius Pilate On the third day Jesus rises from the dead
	40 days later Jesus ascends into heaven
	10 days later the Holy Spirit is poured out on the believers
AD 45	Paul takes the news about Jesus to Asia Minor and Southern Europe
AD 51	Paul writes letters Thessalonica, Corinth, Ephesus and Rome
AD 63 AD 65	Mark's Gospel was written
AD 70 AD 80	Matthew's and Luke's Gospel was written
AD 90 AD 100	John's Gospel was written

These dates are estimated.

Who was Matthew?

Although the writer of the Gospel of Matthew did not identify himself by name, from its earliest days the church has agreed that the author was the apostle **Matthew** (also called Levi). He was a tax collector in Capernaum, before becoming a disciple of Jesus. (Matthew 9:9)

When Jesus called Matthew to follow him, he left everything behind to follow Jesus. Later in this book you will learn how Matthew was keen to introduce others like him to Jesus (Matthew 9:9–13).

THE PURPOSE OF MATTHEW'S GOSPEL

The four Gospels, Matthew, Mark, Luke and John, tell us about the life of Christ. Each has a different emphasis which shows us what was important to the author and his readers. Each Gospel writer or evangelist had a 'target audience' in mind when writing his Gospel.

A Jewish Christian Gospel

Matthew seems to be writing for an audience of Jews and Jewish Christians who were familiar with the Old Testament. We can see this in certain unique features of Matthew's Gospel:

- **Jesus' Jewish background.**

Matthew begins his Gospel with a list of the ancestors of Jesus (this is called a **genealogy**). Ancestors were very important to the Jews, and Matthew wanted to show that Jesus' family could be traced back to many famous figures in Jewish history, including King David and Abraham.

- **Jewish Customs**

Matthew makes reference to Jewish customs, for example hand-washing traditions (15:2) or the wearing of phylacteries (23:5), and did not explain them to his readers. This suggests that his readers were already familiar with Jewish culture.

Many of the issues that Matthew discussed in his Gospel would have been of special interest to Jewish readers: fasting (6:16–180), the Sabbath (12:1–14; 24:20), temple offerings (5:23–24), and the temple tax (17:24–27).

There is a focus on the Law and the Prophets – the foundations of the Jewish faith.

Phylacteries, or *Tefillin*, are small wooden or leather boxes that are strapped to a person's forehead or left arm. Each box holds strips of parchment inscribed with passages from the Jewish scriptures. They are worn in response to Deuteronomy 6:6–8:

> *"Never forget these commands that I am giving you today. Teach them to your children. Repeat them when you are at home and when you are away, when you are resting and when you are working. Tie them on your arms and wear them on your foreheads as a reminder."*

• Language

There is a Jewish influence to some of the Greek that Matthew used.

Where the other Gospels talk about the **Kingdom of God**, Matthew uses the term 'Kingdom of Heaven' after the Jewish tradition of not saying the name of God.

Jewish terms such as 'Son of Abraham' and 'Son of David' are used often.

• Messiah

Matthew wanted to convince his readers that Jesus was the promised Jewish **Messiah**.

This Gospel contains more quotations from the Jewish Scriptures (Old Testament) than any other book of the New Testament– Matthew wants to show that Jesus fulfils prophecy. Examples are the prophecies of Jeremiah 31:15, (see Matthew 2:18), Zechariah 13:7, (see Matthew 26:31) and Isaiah 66:1 (see Matthew 5:35).

Matthew is the only Gospel writer to include Jesus' statements that his mission was limited to *"the lost sheep of the house of Israel"* (10:5–6; 15:24), referring to the Jews.

A Gospel for All Nations

This Gospel is not only for Jewish readers. Matthew does stress that Jesus is the Jewish Messiah, but he also includes many stories and events that suggest that Jesus' mission is also to the Gentiles. For example, the Canaanite woman's faith (15:21–28); the Parable of the Workers in the Vineyard (20:1–16). Matthew's Gospel ends with 'The Great Commission' (28:16–20), where Jesus told his disciples to go into **the whole world** to preach the Gospel.

NOTE

The idea that the Gospel is for the whole world, not just the Jews is called UNIVERSALISM.

The Kingdom of Heaven

In Matthew, the teaching of Jesus is centred on the idea of 'The Kingdom of heaven'. Other Gospel writers refer to it as the Kingdom of God, but the two terms refer to the same thing.

Jesus begins his ministry by declaring:

> *"The Kingdom of heaven is near"* (4:17)

You will explore Jesus' teaching on the Kingdom of God in chapter 4.

FURTHER THINKING

Did you know that each of the Gospel writers has his own symbol? Matthew's symbol is a man. This may be because the Gospel begins with the human genealogy of Jesus or because the Gospel presents Jesus as a 'divine' man. Mark's symbol is a lion, Luke's is a calf and John's is an eagle.
Find out how these other symbols came about.

STYLE

Matthew's Gospel was written carefully and with great skill. Because of the similarities between the two, it seems as though Matthew based his Gospel on Mark's, adding is own stories mainly at the beginning and the end.

The Structure of Matthew's Gospel

Matthew's Gospel is 28 chapters long. Some topics are described in more detail than others which helps the reader to understand what was particularly important to Matthew. Matthew's gospel can be divided in the following way:

- **The prologue** (1:1–2:23).
  This consists of the ancestors of Jesus Christ (genealogy) and birth narrative.

- **The body** (3:1–28:15). This consists of five parts:
  - The Sermon on the Mount (5:1–7:29)
  - The Commissioning of the Apostles (10:1–42)
  - Parables about the Kingdom (13:1–52)
  - Instructions to the Disciples (18:1–35)
  - Final Discourse (24:1–25:46)

Each of these sections ends with a similar closing statement, for example: "*When Jesus had finished saying these things....*" (7:28, 11:1, 13:53, 19:1, 26:1)

- **The Passion Narrative and the Great Commission** (Chapters 26–28)
  This tells the story of Jesus' death, resurrection and ascension.

FOR YOUR FOLDER

1. **Who was Matthew?**
2. **Why did he write his Gospel?**
3. **Why is the Gospel of Matthew much longer than the Gospel of Mark?**
4. **Describe two of the characteristics of Matthew's Gospel.**

Before we look at the important events in the life of Jesus it will be useful to find out as much as possible about the place and time in which he lived. Background information that helps us to understand those events includes the geographical, political, social and religious background of Palestine at the time of Jesus.

PALESTINE AT THE TIME OF JESUS

Geographical Context

Jesus lived in a place called Palestine. Today this land is occupied by the countries of Israel and Palestine. It is an extremely important place for Jews, Christians and Muslims, for whom it has deep, sacred significance.

TIP As you work your way through this book and come across the names of different places it is a good idea to look back to this map to see exactly where the places were.

Key Places in Palestine for a study of the life and ministry of Jesus

The River Jordan

The Jordan River runs from the Uplands of Galilee into the Sea of Galilee, then through the Rift Valley and into the Dead Sea. It splits Palestine down the middle.

The Sea of Galilee

The northern area around **Galilee** is where Jesus spent much of his life. The Sea of Galilee is really a large lake 13 miles long and 7 miles across.

Galilee, Samaria and Judea

Find the **River Jordan** on the map. If you look to the left of it you will see three main regions – **Galilee** at the top, **Samaria** in the middle and **Judea** underneath. It is mainly within these regions that the ministry of Jesus took place, although he does travel beyond them. You may also recognise the place names of some of the towns, where important events happened in the life of Jesus, such as the town of Bethlehem and the city of Jerusalem.

Bethlehem
Bethlehem is a town in Judea where Jesus was born. It was prophesied that the Messiah would be born in the 'town of David': Bethlehem (Micah 5:2).

The Wilderness of Judea
To the east of the Uplands of Judea lies the Wilderness of Judea, a desolate area where John the Baptist lived and where Jesus was tempted.

A scale model of Jerusalem at the time of Jesus.

Jerusalem
Jerusalem was the capital city of Palestine. At the time of Jesus it had a population of about 50,000 people. It was a busy place, with narrow, overcrowded streets and it was part of the main corridor running between Asia and Africa. It had many visitors and the streets were full of traders and travellers, many of whom were Jews who went to visit Jerusalem to carry out their religious duties at festival times.

FURTHER THINKING

Have you ever visited Jerusalem? Do you know what it is like today? Find out 5 facts about the city of Jerusalem.

FOR YOUR FOLDER

Various events in Jesus' life took place in and around Galilee. Referring to the map on page 9, look up the following references and complete the table, writing a sentence on each of them:

Matthew reference	Place	Event in Jesus' life
Matthew 3:1		
Matthew 16:13		
Matthew 13:1		
Matthew 15:21		
Matthew 14:3		
Matthew 26:36		
Matthew 26:57		
Matthew 27:32		

HISTORICAL AND POLITICAL CONTEXT

Palestine was a popular target for invading nations. Its central geographical position made it an important trade route and useful military base. As a result it had been governed by a number of different rulers and influenced by different cultures. For example, from 333BC to 63 BC is known as 'the Greek Period' when many Greek customs were introduced to Palestine. This explains why the New Testament was originally written in Greek.

In 63 BC Palestine came to be under the control of the Romans after General Pompey captured Jerusalem. At the time of Jesus' birth, around 4 BC, the Emperor of the Roman Empire was **Caesar Augustus**. Palestine was governed by **Herod the Great** (37–4 BC).
Herod was an extremely unpopular ruler for a number of reasons:

- He was not a member of the royal family.
- He was only half-Jewish and many Jewish people disliked him because he did not take Judaism seriously.
- He interfered with religious matters. For example, he reduced the power of the **Sanhedrin**, the highest Jewish council. He also reserved the right to appoint or get rid of the **High Priest**.
- He always did as he was told by the Romans and was regarded as a 'puppet-king' and not the true ruler of the Jewish people.
- Herod had a reputation for great cruelty and had ordered the murder of several of his wives and sons. When the army objected to his actions he had 300 soldiers beaten to death.

When Herod died in 4 BC the Jews wanted the Emperor Augustus to end the Herodian rule of Palestine but the Emperor refused and the kingdom was divided between three of Herod's sons:

- Herod Antipas who took charge of **Galilee** and Perea;
- Herod Archelaus who took charge of **Judea and Samaria**; and
- Philip the Tetrarch who took charge of Iturea and Trachonitis. (The map on page 9 shows these territories.)

Out of the three, Archelaus was a brutal, corrupt and incompetent leader. In AD 6 the Romans replaced him with a government official known as a procurator. The procurator answered directly to Rome and was responsible for collecting taxes, keeping the peace and administering justice, which included the power to pass the death sentence. In AD26–36 the procurator was called Pontius Pilate.

The Roman Army

The Roman army was an extremely well organised force. It was highly disciplined, strong, and feared throughout the Roman Empire. As Palestine was occupied by the Romans it was common to see Roman soldiers stationed throughout the country. The soldiers had two main duties to carry out:

- To crush any sign of rebellion against the rule of the Romans
- To make sure that taxes were collected properly

The attitude of the Jews to the Romans varied. Some looked to the benefits that were brought to Palestine, such as good roads, water and sewage systems and magnificent buildings. They also admired the strict system of law and order. Some of these Jews admired the Romans so much that they were prepared to work for them, for example, the Sadducees and the tax collectors.

The majority of the Jewish people despised the presence of the Romans in Palestine and regarded them as bullies, and outsiders in their land. Some Jews (for example, the Zealots) showed their contempt for the Romans through violence and acts of aggression.

The Sanhedrin

The Sanhedrin was the highest Jewish Council in Palestine. There were 71 members made up of religious leaders called Pharisees and Sadducees. It had some power, although it was limited. For example, the Sanhedrin did not have the power to pass the death sentence. The chairman or leader of the Sanhedrin was the High Priest.

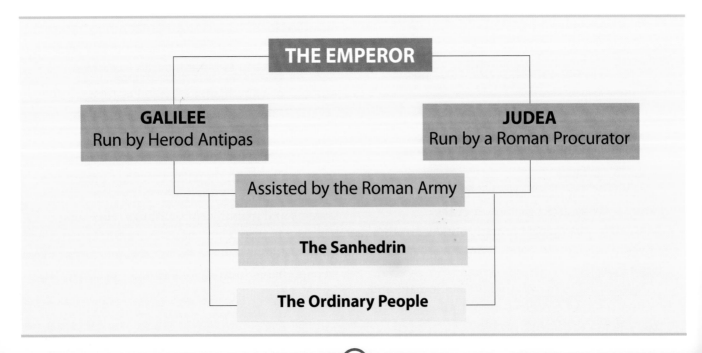

THE EMPEROR

GALILEE
Run by Herod Antipas

JUDEA
Run by a Roman Procurator

Assisted by the Roman Army

The Sanhedrin

The Ordinary People

Tax collectors

Palestine was taxed by the Romans. Local Jewish people worked as tax collectors, gathering money for the Roman government. These people were hated and considered 'sinners' because of what they did:

- They worked for the Roman government, the occupying force in Palestine and therefore were regarded as traitors.
- They had a reputation for being dishonest. It was perfectly normal for tax collectors to charge people a larger amount than was required by the Romans, so they could take a large profit themselves.
- They were not able to give money to charity because it was regarded as 'unclean'.

FOR YOUR FOLDER

1. When did Palestine become part of the Roman Empire?
2. What Emperor ruled the Roman Empire during Jesus' lifetime?
3. Who ruled Palestine at the time of Jesus' birth?
4. How was the Kingdom divided after Herod's death?
5. Explain the attitude the Jews had towards the Romans.
6. Describe some of the duties of the Roman army.
7. Why were tax-collectors not popular people?

RELIGIOUS AND SOCIAL BACKGROUND

The main religion in Palestine at the time of Jesus was **Judaism**. Judaism is one of the oldest monotheistic religions in the world ('monotheism' is the belief that there is only one God).

Covenant

Matthew often refers to the Jewish concept of *covenant*. A covenant is an agreement, promise or contract. In the Old Testament there are three covenants that God made with his people:

- **The Covenant with Noah**.
  You may know the story of Noah and the flood. He built an Ark and was saved from the flood along with his family and two of every kind of creature. God promised that the world would never be destroyed by flood. The sign of this covenant is the rainbow.

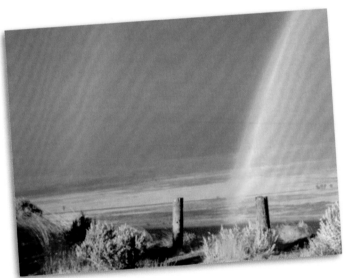

- **The Covenant with Abraham**.
  God made an agreement or covenant with Abraham that he would bless him and make his family a great nation. In response Abraham worshipped and obeyed God.

  The Jews believe that they were chosen from out of all the nations. The sign of this covenant is circumcision. All Jewish boys are circumcised when they are eight days old.

- **The Covenant with Moses.** God gave Moses the Ten Commandments on Mount Sinai for the Jewish people to live by.

Matthew explains that Jesus brings a **New Covenant**. Like the earlier covenants, the New Covenant had a sign – the death of Jesus. Unlike the earlier covenants the New Covenant is open to everyone – not just the Jews. This radical new teaching would prove very unpopular with some people.

The Jewish Law

The first five books of the Old Testament contain the Jewish Law or 'Torah', which were given by God to Moses on Mount Sinai. The Jews' ancestors had promised to keep the law in return for being God's chosen people. Over a thousand years later, at the time of Jesus, the law was still extremely important to the Jews.

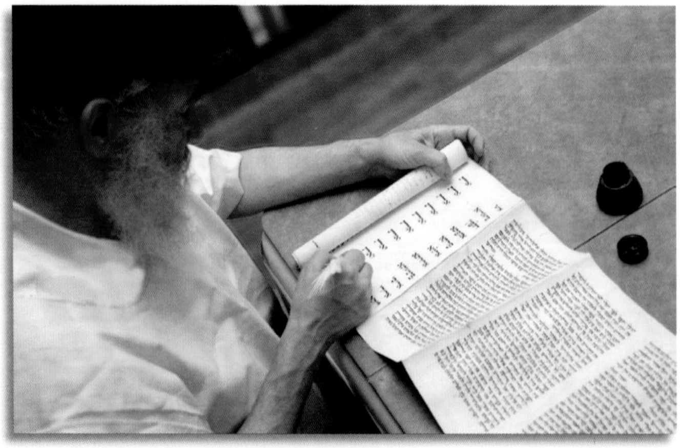

The Jewish religious leaders who interpreted the law were called the **Scribes**. In the Gospels they are often called the 'teachers of the law'. People had great respect for them and would stand up in respect if a Scribe passed by. A lot of discussion took place between the Scribes over the meaning of the law. The interpretation of the law that they agreed upon was called the **Oral Law**. This was a list of complex rules and regulations meant to help people keep the Ten Commandments.

The Sabbath

The word 'sabbath' comes from the Hebrew word *shabat* which means 'to cease'. The Sabbath was a day of rest which began at sunset on Friday evening and lasted until sunset on Saturday evening. All work stopped on the Sabbath day.

Gentiles

A Gentile is anyone who is not Jewish. Many of them worshipped lots of different gods. Some Gentiles were known as 'God-fearers'. They may have followed some Jewish laws or beliefs, but they were not full Jews.

Women

Women had very different lifestyles in first century Palestine compared to women in our society today. Women were second-class citizens and were regarded as inferior to men. Women were viewed as property, first of their father, then of their husband. Girls were not educated like boys. They were usually only trained in household chores like weaving and cooking.

It was considered shameful for a woman to be seen talking to any man apart from her family. Jesus challenges people's attitudes by talking freely with women, treating them with kindness and respect.

FOR YOUR FOLDER

1. What was the main religion of Palestine at the time of Jesus?
2. What is meant by the term 'monotheism'?
3. What is a covenant? Explain, using examples from the Bible.
4. What is a Gentile?
5. Look up the following references and explain what they tell us about the Sabbath:

   Genesis 2:2

   Exodus 20:11

   Numbers 15:32–36
6. Describe the place of women in Jewish society at the time of Jesus.

The Synagogue

A synagogue is a place of worship for Jews. The word 'synagogue' comes from a Greek word meaning 'gathering of people' or 'bringing together'. In Palestine at the time of Jesus there were synagogues in every town that had at least ten men. As well as being a house of prayer, a synagogue was a place of teaching where the scriptures were read and explained. Synagogue services were led and organised by elders. Any Jewish male could be invited to give the sermon, for example, Jesus was often asked to speak in a service (Matthew 4:23). God-fearing Gentiles also attended synagogue worship.

The ruins of the Kfar Bar'am synagogue in upper Galilee.

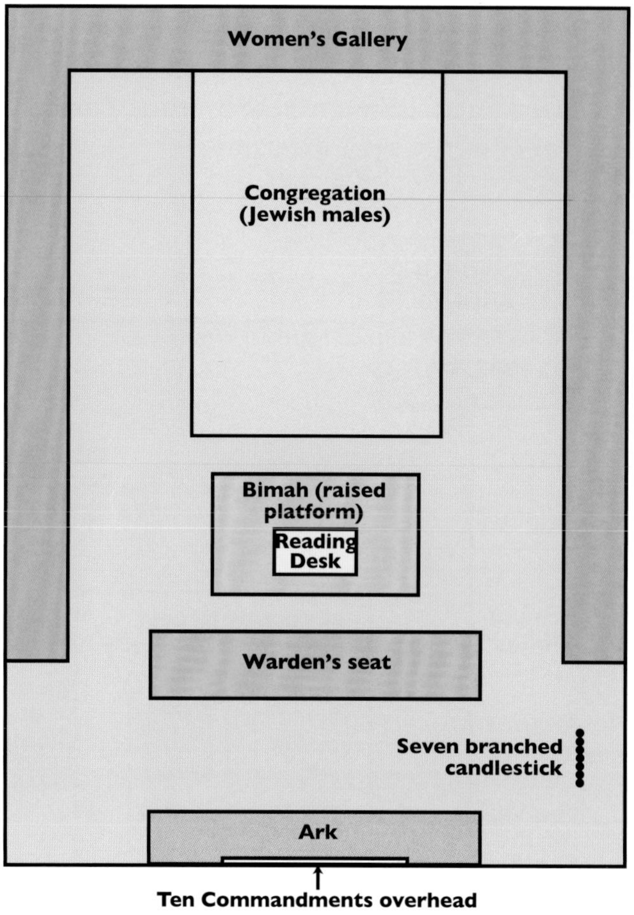

Plan of a synagogue.

The Temple

The first 'temple' to God was a moveable tent called the *Tabernacle*. As the people were wandering in the desert, the temple would go with them (Exodus Chapters 25–27). When the people settled, a permanent Temple was built in Jerusalem by King Solomon. Solomon's temple was later destroyed in a time of war.

At the time of Jesus, Herod the Great was building a new Temple on the original site. It was completely destroyed by the Romans in AD70. All that remains of it now is the western wall, known as the 'Wailing Wall'.

Jews praying at the 'Wailing Wall'

The Temple was important because it was the only place where the Jews could offer sacrifices to God. Sacrifices were made by a priest on the Altar of sacrifice (see diagram).

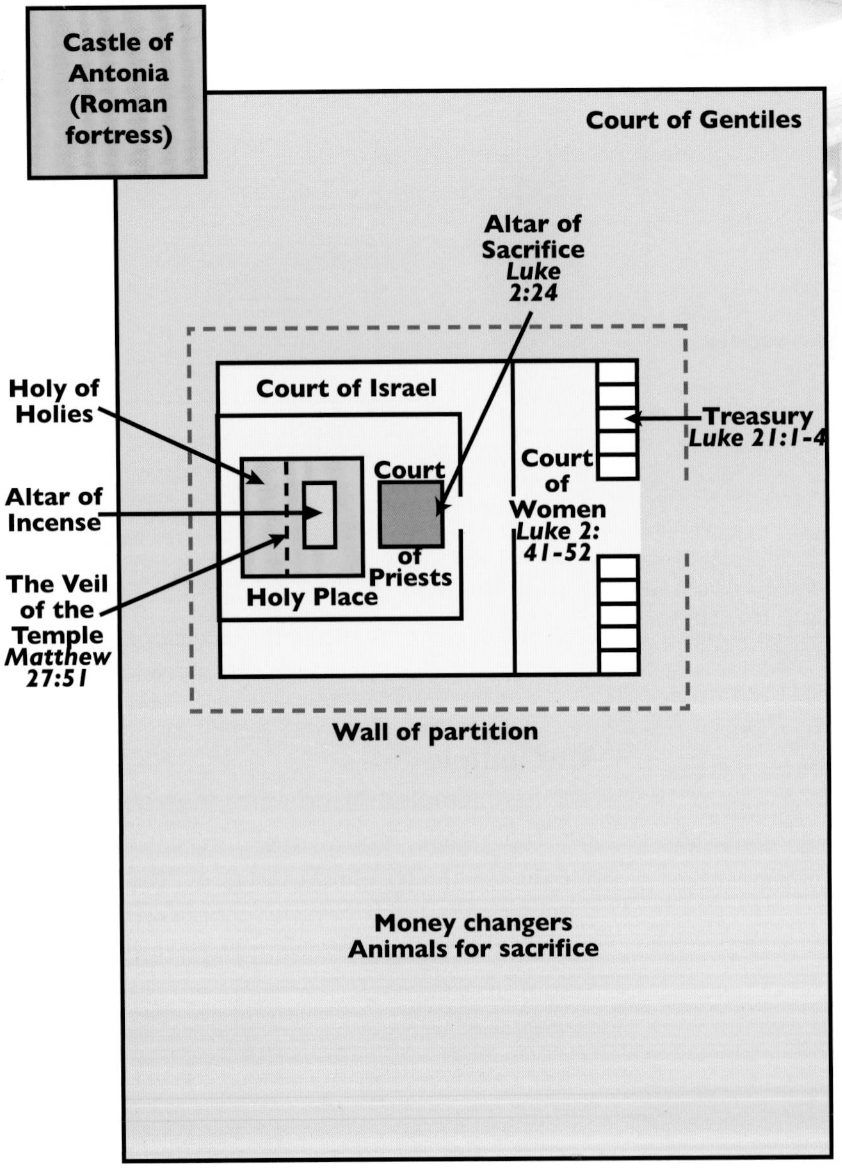

The Temple was spacious and contained one outer court and four enclosed courts:

- **The Outer Court: The Court of Gentiles**

This courtyard was inside the wall of the Temple and was the only part of the Temple grounds that a Gentile (non-Jew) was allowed to enter. Temple markets were held here which catered for worshippers' activities. Money-changers provided suitable coins for the Temple offering: coins with Caesar's head were not allowed. Animals for sacrifice were sold at the Temple markets as they had already been checked for purity by the Temple inspectors.

It was in the Court of the Gentiles that Jesus overturned the tables of the money changers (Matthew 21:12–13).

- **The Court of Women**

Jewish women were allowed to enter this court but were not allowed to go beyond it. The Temple treasury for offerings of money was kept there.

- **The Court of Israel**

This court encircled three sides of the Holy Place. Jewish men were allowed into this court. It was a place where men and priests came to pray.

- **The Holy Place**

The Holy Place was where the Priests could go to burn incense. It was divided into two by a thick curtain called 'The Veil'. Once a year, on the Day of Atonement, the High Priest went beyond the Veil into the Holy of Holies. The Holy of Holies was thought of as the place where God was most present.

FOR YOUR FOLDER

1. What was the synagogue used for apart from religious services?
2. Explain how the Temple was different to the synagogue.
3. List the different courts of the Temple and explain who was allowed to enter each court.
4. What was the altar used for?
5. When was the Temple destroyed?

RELIGIOUS GROUPS WITHIN JUDAISM

The Pharisees

As you learn about the life and ministry of Jesus you will hear a lot about his relationship with the Pharisees and how they opposed Jesus on many occasions. They were the largest and most influential of the religious groups within Judaism in the first century. They lived strictly by the **Oral Law** and were often criticised by Jesus because of this. Jesus believed that many of them did not have genuine faith but were obsessed with keeping petty laws. He often called them hypocrites.
The word *Pharisee* means 'separated one'. They aimed to separate themselves from anything that they believed would make them 'unclean'. This included Romans, Gentiles, and any other Jews who had become 'unclean'.

The Pharisees had a strong belief that a Messiah, or saviour, would come from God to deliver the Jews from their hardships, leading them into a time of religious and political good fortune. They also believed in life after death and bodily resurrection.

The Sadducees

These were a small group of wealthy, upper class religious leaders who looked down on the ordinary people. Most of them were priests. They tried to be friendly with the Romans to keep the power that they held. They opposed any ideas that threatened their privileged position, for example, the expectation of a Messiah. They differed from the Pharisees in that they did not accept the **Oral Law** or the idea of a bodily resurrection after death. However, the Sadducees joined with the Pharisees against Jesus because he criticised them and they saw him as a threat to their relationship with the Romans.

The High Priest

The religious leader of the Jews was the High Priest. He was in charge of the Sanhedrin, the highest Jewish council. Caiaphas was the High Priest at the time of Jesus' death.

The Zealots

The Zealots were a group of Jews who used terrorist tactics against the Romans to gain their religious and political freedom. They were passionate about their beliefs and felt strongly that they should have a land of their own. The Zealots refused to pay taxes and used violence against the Romans.

The Romans refused to tolerate this kind of rebellion and on several occasions they tried to destroy the Zealots. In AD66 the Zealots led a rebellion against the Romans which ended in AD73 when the fortress at Masada was attacked by the Romans. Those inside killed themselves rather than be captured by the Romans. Simon, one of Jesus' disciples, was a Zealot.

The mountain-top fortress at Masada. The Romans could only reach the fortress by building a huge ramp.

The Samaritans

Samaria lay between Galilee and Judea. The people who lived there, the Samaritans, were a mixed race. They were descended from Jews who had intermarried with foreigners when the Assyrians invaded Israel in the eighth century BC, and so they were only partly Jewish.

The Samaritans worshipped the same God as the Jews and accepted some of their Law. The Gospels show us that there was intense hatred between the Jews and the Samaritans (Luke 19:25–37).

FOR YOUR FOLDER

Copy and complete the following table:

Religious Groups	Key Points
Pharisees	
Sadducees	
High Priest	
Scribes	
Zealots	
Samaritans	

Chapter 2

THE IDENTITY OF JESUS

In this section we will be looking at different events in the life of Jesus that give us some insight into who Jesus claimed to be and what people in first century Palestine thought about him.

TITLES OF JESUS

Throughout the Gospel, Matthew uses a number of different 'titles' when referring to Jesus. Each tells us something different about the identity of Jesus.

TIP As you study the Gospel, make a note of the passages where each of these titles is used. It will be useful to give examples in examination.

Son of God

In the Old Testament the king of Israel was sometimes called God's son (Psalm 2:7) but Jesus never used this title to describe himself. Matthew uses the title 'Son of God' at Jesus' baptism (Matthew 3:13–17), and his Transfiguration (Matthew 17:1–13). The title 'Son of God' became a more popular way to describe Jesus after his death and resurrection, and is used widely in the church today.

Christ – Messiah

The Greek word *christ*, and the Hebrew word *messiah*, both mean 'anointed one'. In the Old Testament the word was used for people who were set aside to carry out a special task. High priests and kings were anointed with oil as a sign that God had chosen them.

The Jews believed that a Messiah would come to save them. Some Jews expected the Messiah to be a prophet, like Moses. Others expected a military Messiah who would drive out the Romans and set up a kingdom on Earth for them, restoring the glory of the reign of King David.

Jesus never referred to himself as 'Messiah'. Rather than a powerful military leader, Jesus seems to identify himself with Isaiah's prophecy of a 'suffering servant'. (Isaiah 52:13–53:12) When the disciple Peter described Jesus as the Messiah (Matthew 16:16), he accepted it, but warned the disciples to tell no one.

At various points in his Gospel, Matthew makes it very clear to the reader that Jesus is the Messiah. Examples include: Jesus' baptism (Matthew 3:13–17); Jesus' entry into Jerusalem (Matthew 21:8–11); and the trial before the Sanhedrin (Mathew.26:57–68).

Son of David

King David (1 & 2 Samuel, 1 Kings, 1 Chronicles) was regarded as the greatest king of Israel. During his reign Israel was successful and had its own empire. Most Jews expected that their future Messiah would be a descendant of King David, chosen by God to rule as king. Matthew and Luke, the Gospel writers, trace Jesus' family tree back to David. When people used this title for Jesus in the Gospel stories it shows that they believed him to be the Messiah, for example, the healing of the blind man (Matthew 9:27–31).

Son of Man

Jesus often referred to himself using the title 'Son of Man'. This had two meanings:

Firstly, this title was used by the Old Testament prophet Ezekiel to describe himself. He wanted to show that he was an ordinary person. Likewise, Jesus may have called himself 'Son of Man' to remind his disciples that he was a person like them.

Secondly, 'Son of Man' is used in the prophecy of Daniel 7:13 to describe a figure with authority from God. Many people connected this prophecy with the idea of the coming Messiah.

Jesus used the title 'Son of Man' when he talked about his ministry on earth, when he was talking about his death, and when he spoke about his ascension into heaven.

Saviour

'Jesus' means 'God saves'. The Jews expected a military Messiah who would overthrow their enemies. However, Jesus as Saviour means something else for Christians. Christians believe that Jesus offers salvation to humankind (saves them) through his death and resurrection. This means that Jesus sacrificed himself and took the punishment that was due to humankind.

FOR YOUR FOLDER

Which of the titles given to Jesus do you think would appeal most to people today? Give reasons for your answer.

THE BIRTH OF JESUS MATTHEW 1:18–24

Mary and Joseph were not yet married, but engaged. Engagement at the time of Jesus was considered to be a very serious commitment. Engagements were very rarely broken off. However, as they were not married, and had not had sex, it was a huge shock for Mary to find out that she was pregnant. Joseph must have been horrified. He probably assumed that she had slept with another man. Such behaviour was punishable by death according to the Jewish law.

We can see that Joseph was a kind man because he planned to break off the engagement privately rather than draw unwelcome attention to Mary.

However, Joseph was persuaded to change his mind through a dream where an angel explained to him that Mary's pregnancy was not the result of unfaithfulness on her part, but that the baby had in fact been conceived by the Holy Spirit. The miraculous birth of Jesus is referred to as the 'Virgin Birth'.

NOTE

THE IMPORTANCE OF THE VIRGIN BIRTH
The Gospels tell us that Mary was a virgin when Jesus was born. This means that she never had sexual intercourse. Matthew explains that these events fulfil the prophecy: *"A virgin will become pregnant and have a son, and he will be called Immanuel" (Isaiah 7:14).*

FURTHER THINKING

Mary is an important figure in the Catholic Church. Find out what Catholics believe about the following aspects of Mary's life:

Divine Motherhood

Perpetual Virgin

Immaculate Conception

Assumption

IN A GROUP

Discuss:

Why do you think some people find it difficult to accept the miracle of the virgin birth?

NOTE

INCARNATION
Jesus' birth is described as an 'incarnation' which literally means 'becoming flesh'. It explains the idea that, in Jesus, God took on human form.

VISITORS FROM THE EAST MATTHEW 2:1–12

The next instalment in the story recorded by Matthew took place a few months after the birth of Jesus. You will probably be familiar with the story of Jesus' birth at Bethlehem and the visit of the shepherds as recorded by Luke in his Gospel. Matthew skips over these events and concentrates on the visitors from the east.

Many traditions and stories have grown up around these mysterious visitors. Most people picture them as three wealthy kings who wore the finest of clothes and visited Jesus in a stable alongside the shepherds. You only have to look at a typical nativity set to picture the scene. However, Matthew does not tell us this. The visitors from the east are called *Magi,* **wise men**, not kings.

We have no idea how many of them there were, only that they carried three gifts. And more importantly, they did not arrive to see Jesus until some weeks or months after his birth. By the time of their visit Mary and Joseph had moved into a house (2:11). In the Christian Calendar their visit is celebrated on 6 January and is known as the Feast of the Epiphany.

The wise men have a symbolic role to play in the story of Jesus' birth. Coming from the east, they represent the Gentile (non-Jewish) world coming to worship this new King of the Jews. Jesus had come not just for the Jews but also the Gentiles, and we will see this as the story of Jesus' life unfolds.

The three gifts brought to Jesus by the visitors from the east are also very symbolic. They represent the type of person Jesus would be during his life:

Gold is a precious metal and represents royalty. It emphasises that Jesus is ruler over the Kingdom of God.

Frankincense was a resin taken from a tree and burned for its smell during Temple worship. It represents Jesus' role as a priest, making a link between God and his people.

Myrrh was oil used to anoint the dead. It represents both Jesus' humanity and his death.

When the visitors from the east had arrived in Jerusalem they had tried to get Herod's help to find the child. However, Herod was insulted by the suggestion that there was another 'King of the Jews' and wanted to kill him. He pretended that he also wanted to worship the baby and asked the wise men to tell him if they found the child. However, they were warned in a dream of Herod's real intentions and returned home by a different route.

FOR YOUR FOLDER

1. Who asked 'Where is the baby born to be the King of the Jews?'
2. Why was Herod upset by the visit of the men from the east?
3. Why was it important that Jesus was born in Bethlehem?
4. Explain the significance of the gifts brought by the visitors from the east.
5. Give one reason why Old Testament prophecies were used in the Gospel accounts of Jesus' birth?
6. Explain the meaning of the following terms:

   Incarnation

   Virgin birth

IN A GROUP

In the stories about the birth of Jesus, God spoke through visions and dreams.

Do you think God still speaks to people like this today? Give reasons for your answer.

"People today have forgotten the religious significance of Christmas." Do you agree or disagree? Give reasons for your answer.

THE BAPTISM OF JESUS

MATTHEW 3:1–17

The baptism of Jesus by John the Baptist is recorded in all four Gospels. Matthew describes John the Baptist like an Old Testament prophet. We usually imagine a prophet to be someone who makes predictions about the future. However, in the Bible a prophet was a person who explained the implications of God's word for the present day. Prophets were not always popular people. They were often outspoken and offended people with their message. Likewise, John the Baptist called the religious leaders 'snakes' and said they were like trees which would be cut down and thrown into a fire.

Matthew believed that John was just like the prophet Elijah, that he was a second Elijah. We can see this later on in the words of Matthew 17:12–13:

> *"'But I tell you that Elijah has already come and people did not recognise him, but treated him just as they pleased. In the same way they will also ill-treat the Son of Man.' Then the disciples understood that he was talking to them about John the Baptist."*

Another clue that John was a second Elijah was the way he looked. He dressed almost exactly like Elijah:

> *"He was wearing a cloak made of animal skins, tied with a leather belt,' they answered. 'It's Elijah!" the king exclaimed" (2 Kings 1:8).*

> *"John's clothes were made of camel's hair; he wore a leather belt around his waist and his food was locusts and wild honey" (Matthew 3:4).*

John's role was to announce the Messiah.

> *"John was the man the prophet Isaiah was talking about when he said: "Someone is shouting in the desert, 'Prepare a road for the Lord; make a straight path for him to travel!'"* (Matthew 3:3, see Isaiah 40:3).

John fulfils this prophecy, living in the desert wilderness of Judea and preaching. People came to him to be baptised in the river Jordan.

Baptism was not a new idea. Being ritually cleansed by total immersion in water is a Jewish ritual. John baptised people as a sign of *repentance* – a way of saying sorry to God and making a fresh start in life.

> *"At that time Jesus arrived from Galilee and came to John at the Jordan to be baptised by him" (Matthew 3:13).*

At first John was reluctant to baptise Jesus because he did not feel that he was worthy or good enough to do the job. He also believed that as Jesus was perfect he did not need to repent of sin. Eventually he agreed and the baptism took place. It was accompanied by three important events, which were signs of God's presence:

1. The heavens opened
2. The Spirit of God appeared
3. A voice from heaven spoke

The Spirit of God *"descended like a dove"* (3:16).The voice from heaven (3:17) quoted from Psalm 2:7 and Isaiah 42:1, confirming Jesus' divine identity.

FOR YOUR FOLDER

1. How could John the Baptist be compared to the prophet Elijah?
2. Why do you think John was reluctant to baptise Jesus?
3. What three important events occurred as Jesus was baptised?
4. Why do you think Jesus was baptised?
5. Do you think it is necessary for Christians to be baptised?

IN A GROUP

Discuss the following questions:

– What do you know about the differences between adult and infant baptism?

– Do you think people should be baptised as adults or as infants?

THE TEMPTATIONS OF JESUS

MATTHEW 4:1–11

After Jesus was baptised he took some time to think about what had happened and what was ahead of him in his life. It was important for Jesus to think about how he would use his power to teach people about the Kingdom of God. Matthew tells us that he spent forty days in the desert during which he was tempted by the devil.

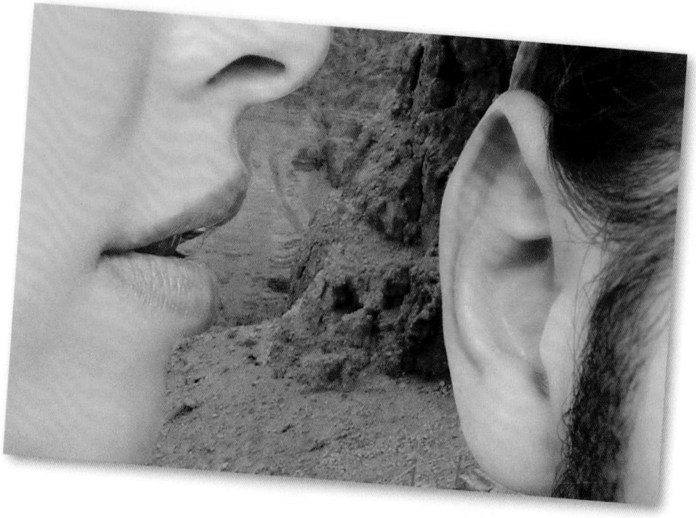

Some people picture the devil as an evil little red man with horns and a tail. However, most Christians regard the temptations that Jesus faced as a mental and spiritual struggle. Faced with each temptation, Jesus had to choose the difficult path, turning his back on the easy options which would have led him to evil.

The three temptations Jesus faces in Matthew's Gospel give us insight into the sort of issues that Jesus was wrestling with during his forty days in the desert.

1. **'Order these stones to turn into bread'**
   The first temptation Jesus faced questioned his ability to perform miracles, and tempted him to use his power selfishly.

   Jesus denied himself the chance to satisfy his hunger, even though he had been fasting and would have been starving. Many people would have been impressed by a miracle that would satisfy their physical hunger, but they would not be following him for his teaching.

   Jesus responds quoting Deuteronomy 8:3, showing that he was not concerned with material things like food for the body, but with spiritual food given by God.

2. **'Throw yourself down'**
In the second temptation Jesus was told to throw himself from the Temple, so that the angels would rescue him. On this occasion the devil quoted scripture (Psalm 91:11–12). He wanted Jesus to misuse his power in order to prove that he was the Messiah and to prove that God loved him. If Jesus carried out spectacular miracles like this he would attract large crowds but they may not have listened to his teaching. Miracles were to be the result of faith in Jesus. Jesus responded to the devil with another quotation from scripture (Deuteronomy 6:16).

3. **'Kneel down and worship me'**
This was a test to see if Jesus would use evil powers to achieve his mission. Would he be able to refuse the chance to have power over the whole earth? Jesus' response to this third temptation shows that he did not see the Messiah as a military or political leader that many Jews expected, but someone who was prepared to put God's kingdom first. Again Jesus used scripture in his response to the devil (Deuteronomy 6:13).

FURTHER THINKING

The season of Lent is linked to the story of Jesus' temptations. Find out why. What do Christians today do during the season of Lent?

Jesus' response shows that he succeeded in fighting against temptation. He was completely obedient to the will of God, even in the face of suffering. Jesus was now prepared to begin his ministry.

IN A GROUP

1. **Make a list of ways in which teenagers are tempted today.**
2. **Do you think that having a religious faith helps a person to deal with temptation?**
3. **"If God will always forgive, then you can give into temptation and do what you want". Do you agree or disagree?**

FOR YOUR FOLDER

1. **Describe each of the temptations of Jesus in the wilderness.**
2. **Why do you think Jesus was tempted?**
3. **To which temptation did Jesus respond 'Do not put the Lord your God to the test'?**
4. **How can Christians learn from Jesus' response to temptation?**
5. **Jesus' responses to the three temptations all came in the form of quotations from the Jewish Scriptures. They were originally commands given to the nation of Israel by God after their escape from Egypt.**

   Look them up for yourself, copy out the following table and fill them in the space provided:

Temptation	Scripture used by Jesus	What does it say?
	Deuteronomy 8:3	
	Deuteronomy 6:16	
	Deuteronomy 6:13	

PETER'S DECLARATION ABOUT JESUS

MATTHEW 16:13–20

An important event took place at Caesarea Philippi which revealed Jesus as the promised Messiah. Jesus openly asked his disciples about his identity. His first question, *"Who do people say the Son of man is?"* (16:13) shows us what the general Jewish public thought: that the Son of Man was John the Baptist, Elijah, Jeremiah or some other prophet. Jesus' second question was directed at his disciples: *"Who do you say that I am?"* (16:15). Peter, who was one of Jesus' closest disciples, was very clear about his opinion: *"You are the Messiah, the Son of the living God"* (16:16).

Caesarea Philippi

Jesus then ordered the disciples not to tell anyone about what had happened.

FOR YOUR FOLDER

1. **Explain the meaning of 'Christ' / 'Messiah'**
2. **Give an account of Peter's declaration about Jesus**
3. **Why do you think it is important for Christians that Jesus was identified as the 'Christ' and not just a good man?**

THE TRANSFIGURATION

MATTHEW 17:1–13

Six days after Peter confessed that Jesus was *"the Messiah, the Son of the Living God"*, a dramatic event called the Transfiguration took place. There are three important things to note:

1. The change in Jesus' appearance:

The word **transfigured** means to be transformed or to change appearance, making something more spiritual or important. At the Transfiguration, Jesus' appearance was changed by becoming *"like the sun"* (17:2).

2. The presence of Moses and Elijah:

Jesus was shown to be equal to the two most important figures in Judaism: Moses and Elijah.

Moses represented the **Law**
Elijah represented the **Prophets**

The Law and the prophets are the foundation of Jewish religion. The appearance of Moses and Elijah communicates that Jesus fulfilled their prophesies, and his teaching fulfilled the Law.

It was believed that figures from the scriptures would appear in the lead up to the end of the world.

3. The cloud and the voice:
A shining cloud also came from above and a voice spoke from the cloud, confirming that Jesus was the Son of God. In Jewish scripture a cloud was a symbol of God's presence (Exodus 24:15–18; 40:34). The words spoken were similar to those at Jesus' baptism (see page 22).

Peter suggested marking the place where the Transfiguration had taken place by building three tents for Jesus, Moses and Elijah. This was a Jewish custom to remember the great figures of Judaism. Jews today still celebrate the 'Feast of Tabernacles'.

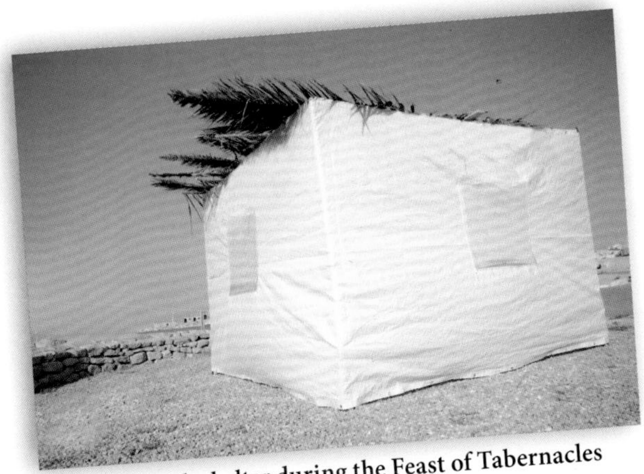
A Jewish shelter during the Feast of Tabernacles

Jesus warned the disciples not to tell anyone about the Transfiguration until the Son of Man (Jesus) had risen from the dead. This is similar to the occasions when Jesus told people not to tell others about his miracles. There would come a time, after his death, when the significance of the Transfiguration would be understood.

FOR YOUR FOLDER

1. **Name the Old Testament characters who appeared with Jesus at the Transfiguration and explain their significance.**
2. **Name another occasion when God said he was pleased with Jesus.**
3. **Why do you think the Transfiguration was important for the disciples?**

NOTE

'THE SECRET MESSIAH'
The Gospels often present Jesus as a secretive and mysterious figure. He teaches his disciples in secret and he orders those he has healed not to tell anyone. He commands demons to be quiet when they begin to announce his identity, and his disciples fail to understand who Jesus really is.

Jesus may not have wanted people to know from the start that he was the Messiah because the people were expecting a strong leader who would drive out their enemies, the Romans. Jesus knew that as the Messiah he must suffer and die. His disciples witnessed his miracles and listened to his teaching and identified him as the Messiah, but even they did not expect him to be put to death.

JESUS' ENTRY INTO JERUSALEM

MATTHEW 21:1–11

Jesus makes his way to the city of Jerusalem. He had predicted that he would suffer and die there (16:21-28). In the Christian Church today this is remembered as 'Palm Sunday', and it marks the beginning of the final week of Jesus' life.

Throughout Jesus' ministry he cautioned his followers many times not to tell anyone about miracles he performed and it seemed he wanted to keep his true identity as Messiah a secret. Now that had changed. Rather than avoiding attention, Jesus made a grand entrance into the city.

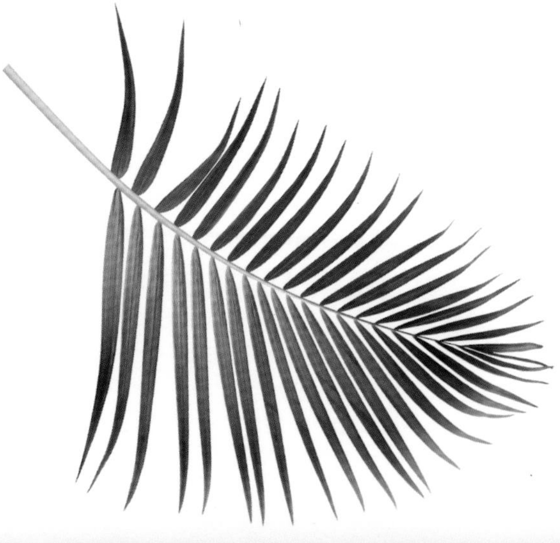

Jesus was confirming his true identity as:

- **a popular figure** – Jesus was popular with the ordinary people. They did not regard him as a hypocrite, like other religious leaders.
- **a humble servant** – Jesus rode on a colt (a young male donkey), not a horse as a king would have done. Jesus was entering Jerusalem as a servant.
- **the 'Son of David'**– the Messiah predicted in the Jewish scriptures.
- **'Lord'** (21:3) – This is the only place in Matthew's Gospel where Jesus used the title 'Lord' of himself.

Jesus deliberately fulfilled Zechariah's prophecy:

"Tell the city of Zion, Look, your king is coming to you! He is humble and rides on a donkey and on a colt, the foal of a donkey" (Zechariah 21:5) .

Zion was a poetic name for Jerusalem and the Jews believed that Jerusalem belonged to the Messiah (Matthew 5:35). The crowds showed that they believed Jesus was the Messiah by spreading their clothes on the road and throwing palm branches before him. They sang words of praise which come from Psalm 118:25–26. 'Hosanna' means 'save now!', but it was commonly used as a word of praise. It was an amazing scene of great celebration.

FOR YOUR FOLDER

1. **What title did the crowds use for Jesus as he entered Jerusalem?**
2. **Whose prophecy did Jesus fulfil?**
3. **Jesus entered Jerusalem on a donkey, symbolising peace, rather than the military power of a horse. How do you think Christians could follow Jesus' example in their lives today?**

Chapter 3

JESUS THE MIRACLE WORKER

Jesus' miracles have been a topic for debate for many people. The key questions that people ask are:

> *"Were they actual supernatural events?"*
>
> *"Did they just seem to be miraculous when, in reality, they had a logical and scientific explanation?"*

Matthew was writing at a time when many people believed in the power of miracles. He did not try to explain the miracles by giving a detailed scientific account of them. His aim was not to prove that a particular event was a miracle but to show the amazing way in which God worked through Jesus.

A LEPROSY SUFFERER

MATTHEW 8:1–4

At the time of Jesus the skin disease known as 'leprosy' was common. Strict instructions were given in the Jewish scriptures to help prevent the spread of such diseases (see Leviticus 13:45–46). Leprosy is not a contagious disease but people thought it was, which meant that 'lepers' were treated as social outcasts.

Jesus showed great compassion to the man, not only by healing him but by touching him. Jewish people would have been shocked at this because they believed that contact with lepers would make a person 'unclean'. Jesus was not happy with this misconception. He did not like the fact that the Jewish law separated someone from society because they had been pronounced unclean.

The leper showed that he had great faith in Jesus' ability to heal him when he said to Jesus *"Sir, if you want to, you can make me clean"* (8:2) Afterwards Jesus advised the man to go and show himself to the priest for examination. The priest was the only one who had the authority to declare a person clean again. Jesus told the healed man not to tell anyone else about the miracle.

FOR YOUR FOLDER

1. **Explain how people with leprosy were regarded at the time of Jesus.**
2. **Why was Jesus' treatment of this man out of the ordinary?**
3. **How did the man in this story impress Jesus?**
4. **How could Christians today learn from Jesus' attitude towards 'lepers'?**

NOTE

The Leprosy Mission

THE LEPROSY MISSION

What is Leprosy?
Leprosy is a mildly infectious disease caused by a tiny rod like germ called *Mycobacterium leprae* which can damage the nerves under the skin. Untreated it can lead to loss of feeling in hands, feet and face. With the loss of feeling and absence of pain injuries can occur leading to disability.

Can it be cured?
Leprosy can be cured in as little as 6 months using multi-drug therapy.

Who has Leprosy?
Leprosy can affect people of all ages and social backgrounds although 90% of all cases occur in less developed areas of the world.

How do people get Leprosy?
Leprosy is not passed on by touch, drinking dirty water, or sharing food with someone who has leprosy, nor is it hereditary. It is thought an infected person passes it on by coughing and sneezing.

What is The Leprosy Mission?
The Leprosy Mission is an international Christian charity which works in over 28 countries worldwide to provide help to those affected by leprosy.

What does The Leprosy Mission do?
The Leprosy Mission provides medical services, education scholarships, work training, low cost housing, small business loans and business training. The Mission's aim is to restore leprosy patients' health, independence and self respect.

FURTHER THINKING

Find out about the work of an organisation that reaches out to outcasts in our society. Examples of outcasts may include:

- **Alcoholics**
- **Drug addicts**
- **Gamblers**

A ROMAN OFFICER'S SERVANT

MATTHEW 8:5–13

One of the main features of Matthew's Gospel is its message that God is for everyone, both Jews and Gentiles. The miracle of the healing of the Roman officer's servant is an example of this.

The Jews believed that they were God's chosen people. This miracle would have upset some, and challenged their attitudes. The Roman officer was a Gentile, a non-Jew, although he had great respect for Judaism. He was probably a God-fearer (someone who was interested in Judaism but had not become a full Jew ie. had not been circumcised).

It is clear that the Roman officer was a kind man because he cared about the health of his servant. At the time of Jesus slaves and servants had no rights at all and were generally not treated very well. It would have been very unusual for them to get help if they became ill. However, the Roman officer was different and asked Jesus for help when his servant became ill.

The Roman officer's attitude towards Jesus is interesting. Because of his position in the army he would have been used to giving orders. However, he clearly recognised that Jesus had a much greater authority than he had, an authority which came from God. Jesus praised him for his faith:

> "I tell you, I have never found anyone in Israel with faith like this" (8:10)

As a result, the servant was healed. The faith of the Roman officer was greater than any that Jesus had seen among the Jewish people.

Jesus' spoke about the messianic banquet that was prophesied in the Jewish scriptures (Isaiah 25:6–9). He used this image to emphasis that the Kingdom of God is open to all, both Jews and Gentiles. However, he also explained that there will be some who will be rejected from the kingdom. This would have shocked many of his listeners who would have expected to be part of the Kingdom of God simply because they were born Jewish. Jesus teaches that entrance to the Kingdom of God depends on genuine faith, such as that demonstrated by the Roman officer's servant.

FOR YOUR FOLDER

1. **Explain what type of person the Roman officer was.**
2. **Why would some of the people have been annoyed by Jesus' actions and comments ?**
3. **Why was the servant healed?**
4. **Do you think the Christian Church does enough to challenge prejudice and discrimination in our society?**
5. **'You do not have to have religious faith to believe that miracles happen.' Do you agree or disagree?**

A PARALYSED MAN

MATTHEW 9:1–7

On this occasion Jesus healed a paralysed man. Some people brought the man to Jesus on a bed. Jesus was clearly touched by the faith of these people because he said to the man, *"Courage, my son! Your sins are forgiven"* (9:2). At the time of Jesus many people associated illness with having committed sin.

The Pharisees standing near must have been shocked because they considered his words to be blasphemy (9:3). They believed that only God could forgive sins, so in their opinion Jesus was claiming to be equal with God. Imagine their outrage.

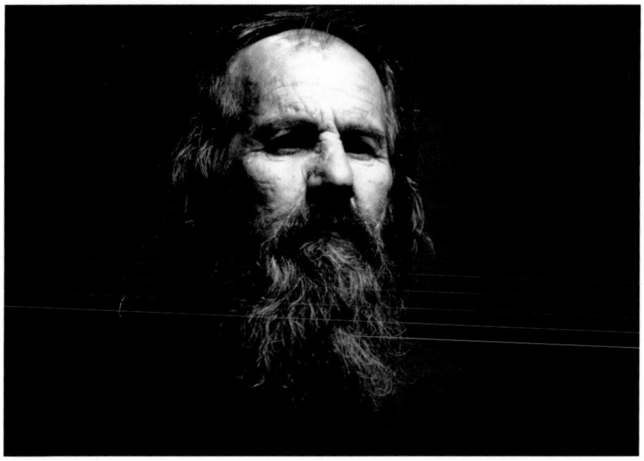

Jesus knew exactly what they were thinking and announced: *"I will prove to you, then, that the Son of Man has authority on earth to forgive sins"* (9:6). You will notice that this is one of the occasions where Jesus calls himself **'Son of Man'.** He then told the paralysed man to pick up his bed and go home. The people who saw this miracle were so amazed that they praised God for giving such authority to people.

FOR YOUR FOLDER

1. **What did Jesus say when he saw the faith of the friends of the paralysed man?**
2. **Why would the Pharisees have been furious about this?**
3. **Explain why Jesus may have called himself 'Son of Man' on this occasion.**
4. **How might Christians today be influenced by Jesus' attitude to the sick?**

FURTHER THINKING

Do you think it is important for Christians to believe that miracles really happen? Discuss in a small group.

AN OFFICIAL'S DAUGHTER AND A WOMAN

MATTHEW 9:18–26

Jesus was approached by a Jewish official from the local synagogue. He was distraught because his daughter had just died and he begged Jesus to bring her back to life. Such was Jesus' reputation as a miracle worker that the official had faith that Jesus could do this.

Jesus followed him immediately but was side-tracked along the way by a woman who had suffered from severe bleeding for twelve years. In the eyes of the Jewish law, her condition made her ceremonially unclean, preventing her from joining in Jewish festivals and ceremonies. She was obviously ashamed and tried to touch Jesus' cloak secretly, in the hope that this action would cure her. Clearly, like the Jewish official, she had great faith.

Jesus was fully aware of what was happening and praised the woman: 'Courage, my daughter! Your faith has made you well.' Jesus' reaction to this woman was unusual in a society where men were regarded as superior. Not only did he speak to the woman, but he addressed her using a term of deep respect. He also wanted the woman to know that her faith had played a part in making her well. Faith is the key to understanding both of these miracles.

Afterwards Jesus went to official's house where people had gathered in mourning and preparations were being made for the child's funeral. The crowd laughed when Jesus claimed that the child was not dead, but sleeping. Jesus insisted that they leave the room and he then took the girl's hand and she got up. The news of this miracle spread around the whole area.

The healing of the official's daughter shows that Jesus had power over death.

FOR YOUR FOLDER

1. **Jesus met a woman on the way to the Jewish official's house. Why would she have been ashamed of her condition?**
2. **What did Jesus tell this woman about why she was healed?**
3. **What happened when Jesus reached the official's house?**
4. **Do you think that Jesus had power over death? Give reasons for your answer.**

A MAN WITH A PARALYSED HAND

MATTHEW 12:9–14

Some of the Pharisees wanted to accuse Jesus of doing wrong, so they asked him if he thought it was against the Jewish Law to heal on the Sabbath. The Pharisees taught that you could give medical assistance on the Sabbath only if someone's life was in danger. Jesus claimed the right to heal on the Sabbath to help someone in need. Jesus reasoned that the Pharisees would rescue one of their sheep from a pit on the Sabbath, and the life of a person is superior to that of an animal (see also 6:26 and 10:31). Jesus then healed the man, saying *"Stretch out your hand"*(12:13). Notice that on this occasion Matthew makes no mention of the faith of the healed man. Having failed to trick Jesus, the Pharisees left and made plans to kill him.

IN A GROUP

Do you believe miracles happen today in the same way as described in Matthew's Gospel?
Give reasons for your answers, showing that you have looked at different points of view.

FURTHER THINKING

"Jesus healed on the Sabbath. The Christian idea of keeping Sunday special is outdated."
Discuss this statement.

FOR YOUR FOLDER

1. What did the Pharisees believe about helping people on the Sabbath?
2. How did Jesus justify healing on the Sabbath?
3. Explain why Jesus' words and actions would have angered the Pharisees.

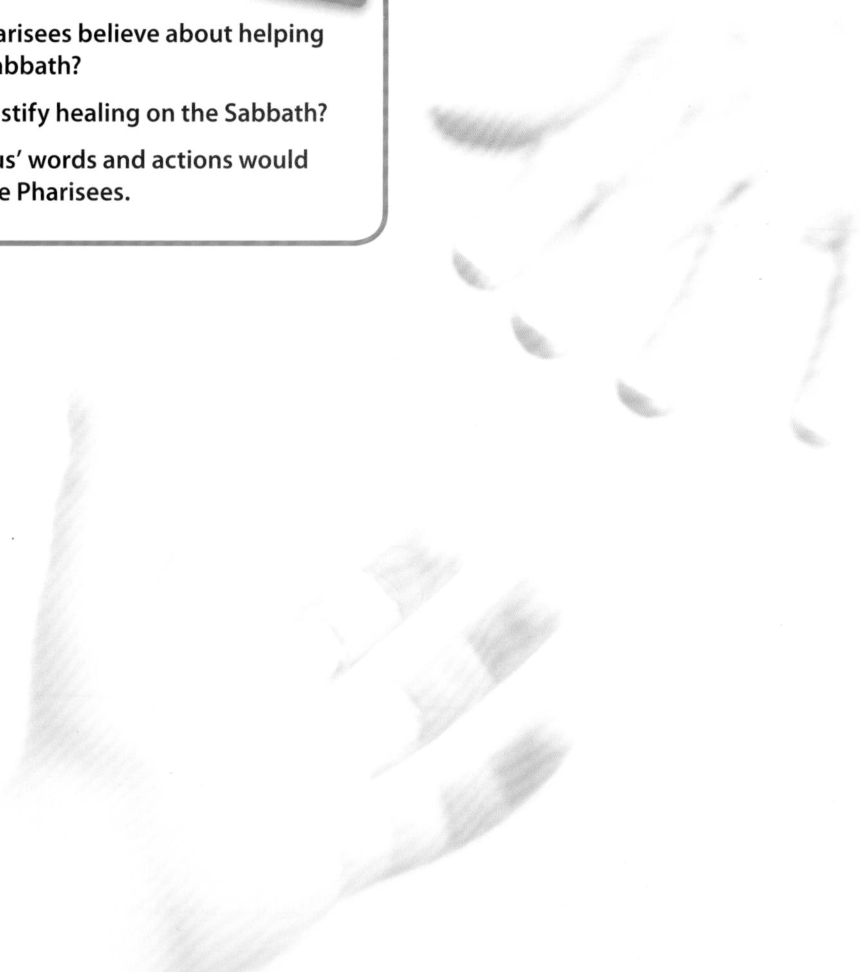

Chapter 4

THE KINGDOM OF GOD

When you hear the word 'kingdom' you might think of a geographical place. You might be reminded of fairy tales that you were told as a child, or think of a place like the United Kingdom.

When the Bible talks about the 'Kingdom of God' it doesn't refer to a geographical kingdom, or to a place somewhere up in the sky. Jesus' understanding of the Kingdom of God was that it was a group of people: those who regarded God as their king.

When Jesus began his ministry in Galilee he preached using the words:

> "*Turn away from your sins, because the Kingdom of heaven is near*" (Matthew 4:17).

What Jesus meant was that God's rule or kingdom had come. Note that Matthew usually referred to the Kingdom of God as the 'Kingdom of heaven'. This is probably because Matthew was a Jew and wanted to avoid using God's name out of respect for the third commandment. However, they both refer to the same thing.

PARABLES

A parable is a story that illustrates a spiritual truth about the Kingdom of God. Jesus used parables to teach his followers.

Jesus' disciples asked him why he used parables when he talked to people. Jesus explained that through parables those who wanted to know more about God's kingdom would progress to understand more. Those who had closed their minds and their hearts to God would never understand even a little.

Jesus used parables to teach the people for the following reasons:

1. They were a common method used by many teachers or *rabbis* at that time.

2. A parable was easy to understand.

3. Parables challenged people to work out the meaning for themselves. People would have enjoyed listening and trying to discover the hidden meaning.

4. Jesus used everyday situations in his parables. It showed the people that he was on their level and understood their lives.

The parables in Matthew's Gospel usually begin with the words: 'The Kingdom of heaven is like this...' Matthew's parables often bring out royal imagery or scenes of judgement, with rewards for the righteous and punishments for the wicked. For example, in the Parable of the Wedding Feast the wrongdoer goes to the place of *"weeping, wailing and gnashing of teeth"* (22:1–16)

In the Parable of the Sheep and the Goats there is a great separation on the Day of Judgement, and rewards and punishments are assigned on the basis of whether or not people have fed the hungry, clothed the naked and visited those in prison. (25:31–46)

In Matthew 13, Jesus tells seven parables of the Kingdom. We are going to look at two of them in detail, the Parable of the Sower (13:1–23) and the Parable of the Weeds (13:24–43).

Allegories

Some of the parables told by Jesus are also classed as 'allegories'. An allegory is a type of parable where the characters and events in the story all represent real people and events. This means that every detail in the allegory has a meaning, unlike a parable which makes one simple point. An example of an allegory is the Parable of the Sower.

FURTHER THINKING

1. **Discuss what the difference is between a parable and an allegory.**
2. **In pairs explain why parables were a popular teaching method.**

NOTE

Jesus was a teacher (*rabbi*) who tried to get God's message across to the ordinary people. His teaching can be described as being both practical and challenging and he used relevant stories and themes to keep his audiences interested.

Jesus' teaching was not only relevant for the first century but can also be applied to life in the twenty-first century.

THE PARABLE OF THE SOWER

MATTHEW 13:1–9, 18–23

The Parable of the Sower is a clear example of a parable or allegory about the Kingdom of God. It is one of the most famous parables told by Jesus.

Matthew writes about this parable in three parts:

- **Chapter 13:1–9:**
The Parable of the Sower, which Jesus told to a large crowd

- **Chapter 13:10–17*:**
Jesus explains the purpose of parables to his disciples

- **Chapter 13:18–23**
Jesus explains the parable of the sower to his disciples

*not on GCSE course

As well as having meaning for the listeners of Jesus' day the parable of the Sower has a clear message for people today. The following diagram explains the meaning of the Parable of the Sower:

THE PARABLE	MEANING	SIGNIFICANCE FOR TODAY
"Once there was a man who went out to sow corn." (13:3)	**Man** God **Seed** The Word of God	The parable teaches what will happen when the Word of God is proclaimed. The Word of God is like seed which is planted and starts to grow. If people listen to God's word they will grow in a spiritual way.
"As he scattered the seed in the field some of it fell along the path and the birds ate it up." (13:4)	**Path** "Those who hear the message about the Kingdom but do not understand it." (13:19) **Birds** "The Evil One comes along and snatches away what was sown in them." (13:19)	Some people are distracted from taking the Christian faith seriously. Can you think of some things that might distract people?
"Some of it fell on the rocky ground, where there was little soil. The seeds soon sprouted, because the soil wasn't deep. But when the sun came up, it burnt the young plants; and because the roots had not grown deep enough, the plants soon dried up." (13:5–6)	**Rocky ground** "Those who receive the message gladly as soon as they hear it. But it does not sink deep into them, and they don't last long." (13:20–21) **Sun** "So when trouble or persecution comes along because of the message, they give up at once." (13:22)	Some people are attracted by Christianity until they realise what it means to be a Christian, that it requires a deep commitment. **What sort of changes might someone have to make to be a Christian?**
"Some of the seed fell among the thorn bushes, which grew up and choked the plants." (13:7)	**Thorn bushes** "Those who hear the message; but the worries about life and the love for riches choke the message and they don't bear fruit." (13:22)	Some people let worries ruin God's influence on their lives. **What sort of worries might they have?** The 'thorns' can be compared to greed, anger or jealousy, all of which choke spiritual growth.
"But some seed fell in good soil, and the plants produced corn, some produced a hundred grains, others sixty, and others thirty." (v13:8)	**Good soil** "Those who hear the message and understand it: they bear fruit, some as much as a hundred, others sixty, others thirty." (13:23)	A few people will accept the Gospel message and stay firm in their faith, in spite of difficulties which they may face. They will continue to grow as Christians, carrying out God's purpose in their lives.

IN A GROUP

Discuss the different ways in which people respond to the Gospel message today.
What distractions prevent people from becoming Christians?

THE PARABLE OF THE WEEDS

MATTHEW 13:24–30, 36–43

In this parable it is the *seed* and not the *ground* that is the focus of the story. The sower sows good wheat seeds in a field, but while his men are sleeping his enemy comes and sows the seed of weeds as well. This weed was probably 'darnel', a plant that looks like wheat when the plants are young. Matthew explains that the enemy thoroughly planted the darnel seed among the young wheat. The roots would have intertwined with the roots of the wheat and when the two plants grew to maturity it became obvious what the enemy had done.

Jesus later explained his parable as an allegory: The field is the world; the Sower is the 'Son of Man' (Jesus); the enemy is the devil; the good seed is people who belong to the Kingdom; the weeds are the *"sons of the evil one"* (13:38); the harvest workers are angels; and the time of harvest is the end of the age.

The parable shows that in the world both 'wheat' and 'weeds' are allowed to grow together. This means that believers and unbelievers will be together and will not be separated until the end of the age. At that time the 'wheat' will be gathered into the barn and the 'weeds' bundled up and burned.

FOR YOUR FOLDER

Copy and complete the following table explaining the Parable of the Weeds:

Symbolism in the Parable of the Weeds	
Sower	
Field	
Good seed	
Weeds	
Enemy	
Harvest	
Workers	
Fiery furnace	

FURTHER THINKING

Some Christians believe that this parable suggests Satan will do anything to prevent the growth of the Kingdom of God. Can you list some ways in which Christianity is prevented from spreading today?

THE PARABLE OF THE WORKERS IN THE VINEYARD

MATTHEW 20:1–16

Jesus told the story of the workers in the vineyard to help his listeners understand what the Kingdom of heaven is like. Early one morning the owner of a vineyard hired some men to work and agreed to pay them the going rate, which was a silver coin for a day's work. At various times throughout the day the man hired more workers for his vineyard. He did not promise them a particular wage, only that he would deal fairly with everyone.

The Law of Moses explained that workers were to be paid at the end of the day so that they could buy food for their families (Deuteronomy 24:15; Leviticus 19:13). So at the end of the day all the workers were brought together to be paid, starting with those who had been hired last. Everyone was given one silver coin. But the men who had been hired at the start of the day were unhappy about this and argued that they had done more work than the others. The owner of the vineyard refused to accept this. He pointed out that they had agreed to receive a silver coin for the day's work and that is what they had got. If the owner wanted to be generous to those hired later in the day that was his own business:

> *"Don't I have the right to do as I wish with my own money? Or are you jealous because I am generous?"* (20:15).

This parable suggests that people should have a right attitude in serving God and should not be looking for a reward for good deeds. Christians should not compare themselves to others, but trust God to deal with each person as he wishes. The story explains that those who consider themselves to be least important in the Kingdom of heaven will be the most important because rewards in the kingdom are not based on people's actions but on God's grace.

Some Christians believe that the twelve disciples correspond to the workers hired at the beginning of the day, the beginning of Jesus' ministry. Those hired later correspond to other people who became followers of Jesus later on. God has the right to give just as great reward to those whose service is not as long. In some cases the last called will be among the first to receive blessing.

FOR YOUR FOLDER

1. **Why were some of the workers in the vineyard unhappy when it came to being paid for what they had done?**
2. **How did the owner of the vineyard justify his actions?**
3. **Explain how this parable can be compared to service in the Kingdom of God.**
4. **Do you think some Christians, for example ministers, priests and missionaries deserve a greater reward than others?**

THE PARABLE OF THE WEDDING FEAST

MATTHEW 22:1–14

Jesus told a parable using the familiar setting of a wedding party, but the events of this story cause some surprising reactions. The parable is an example of universalism, which is the idea that the Gospel is for all people, Jews and Gentiles.

A man was preparing a wedding feast for his son and sent his servants to bring the invited guests. But they did not want to come. So he sent more servants with the message:

> *"My feast is ready now; my steers and prize calves have been butchered, and everything is ready. Come to the wedding feast!"*

The guests reacted in different ways. Some ignored the servants and went about their own business. Others reacted violently and beat the servants and killed them. Furious, the king sent soldiers to kill these murderers. The king decided that the original guests did not deserve to be at the wedding feast. So he sent his servants on to the streets to invite people. Good and bad alike came to the feast.

However one man was not wearing a suitable outfit. The king was disgusted that he had not made the effort and had him thrown out, into the dark: *"There he will cry and gnash his teeth"* (22:13).

Jesus concluded: *"Many are invited, but few are chosen"* (22:14).

This table summarises the meaning of the parable:

WEDDING FEAST	Kingdom of heaven	A reference to salvation; being part of the community of God; everlasting life.
ORIGINAL GUESTS	Jews	The Jews, because of national pride, had come to believe that being a Jew was all that was needed to enter the Kingdom of heaven. Jesus taught something different – The Kingdom was open to everybody.
NEW GUESTS	Gentiles	God would allow anyone to enter the kingdom, not just the Jews. God's servants would go out into the world to invite as many as would to come.
UNSUITABLY DRESSED MAN	Unprepared for commitment	This may point to the importance of being fully prepared for complete commitment in Christ.

FOR YOUR FOLDER

1. **What happened when it came time for the wedding feast?**
2. **What did the king do as a result of his anger?**
3. **Describe what happened to the guest who was not dressed properly.**
4. **Explain how this parable is an example of universalism.**

THE PARABLE OF THE SHEEP AND THE GOATS

MATTHEW 25:31–46

Matthew stressed judgment many times in his Gospel (3:12; 13:49-50; 22:14; 24:51; 25: 30). The Parable of the Sheep and the Goats is an example of this. Just as the wheat and the weeds could not be separated until judgment day, so it is with the sheep and the goats in this parable.

In the parable the king (God) is the judge. The people of all nations are brought before him to be judged according to their actions. They are divided in the same way that a shepherd separates the sheep from the goats (in Palestine, sheep and goats look quite alike). The people are divided into two groups:

Righteous (sheep) – on his right
Unrighteous (goats) – on his left

This parable reinforces the importance of *doing* what God wants and not just *talking* about it. When Jesus described the 'sheep' as 'righteous', he was showing that true faith in God has implications for how Christians should live their lives. An example of a righteous life is helping others when they are in need. For example, a righteous person will want to help other people whenever they can. The parable shows that when people serve others it is as if they are serving Jesus himself.

The unrighteous in the parable were described as those who did not help others when they had the opportunity. Therefore the parable also shows that people will be judged by their motives and attitudes.

FOR YOUR FOLDER

1. **Explain the symbolism of the 'sheep' and the 'goats'.**
2. **Name four good actions that were praised by the King.**
3. **What does the parable teach Christians about the Day of Judgment?**
4. **What similarities are there between the Parable of the Weeds and the Parable of the Sheep and the Goats?**
5. **Using this parable, explain how someone would act if they followed the teaching of Jesus.**

Chapter 5

THE DEATH AND RESURRECTION OF JESUS

The importance of Jesus' death and resurrection to the Gospel writers is enormous. While only two of them (Matthew and Luke) record Jesus' birth, all four describe in detail the events surrounding Jesus' death and resurrection. In Matthew's Gospel seven out of the twenty-eight chapters are taken up with what is known as the 'Passion narrative'.

The word *passion* means 'suffering'. The term 'passion of Christ' is commonly used at Easter time to describe the suffering Jesus endured.

Why would people wear a symbol of execution around their neck?

Jesus' death was inevitable. However, it still brought immense sadness and distress to his followers. Looking back, Christians can celebrate that because of Jesus' death the offer of salvation is open to all people. It is interesting that Christianity is the only religion that actively celebrates its founder's death. Through Jesus' resurrection he defeated the power of evil and death. Jesus' death and resurrection are central to the Christian faith.

In this section we will look at the events surrounding the death and resurrection of Jesus and consider their significance for the Christians.

THE PLOT AGAINST JESUS MATTHEW 26:3–15

Opposition to Jesus had been building up for some time. Matthew describes how Jesus' enemies, the chief priests and the elders, meet in secret to finalise the plot to kill him. They met together in the house of Caiaphas, the High Priest, but were wary of arresting Jesus during the Passover in case there was a riot. Many pilgrims from Galilee and the Diaspora (Jews who lived outside Palestine) were present in Jerusalem for the Passover celebrations.

Jesus was in Bethany at the house of Simon, a healed leper, with his disciples and some others. While Jesus was eating, a woman (John 12:3 says it was Mary, the sister of Lazarus) came to him with an alabaster jar filled with an expensive perfume, which she poured on his head. We know from the account in John's Gospel that the perfume cost about one year's wages (John 12:3–5). The disciples were angry at the apparent waste:

> *"This perfume could have been sold for a large amount and the money given to the poor!"* (26:9)

There is a sharp contrast between the woman's generosity and the poor attitude of those who criticised her. They failed to appreciate that this anointing of Jesus was symbolic. The word *messiah* means 'anointed one'. A king would be anointed before his coronation, and the dead were anointed before they were buried. The woman's anointing of

Jesus was a sign of his coming death.

Jesus defended the woman's actions and used the situation to hint to his disciples what was about to happen: his crucifixion.

> *"It is a fine and beautiful thing that she has done for me. You will always have poor people with you, but you will not always have me."* (26:10–11).

Jesus then predicted that the woman's anointing would become part of the Gospel story which would be preached in the whole world.

JUDAS AGREES TO BETRAY JESUS

MATTHEW 26:14–16

Judas Iscariot went to the chief priests and asked, *"What will you give me if I betray Jesus to you?"* (26:15). Nobody knows why Judas decided to betray Jesus. Whatever the reason, Judas found his proposal was welcomed by the religious leaders. They counted out thirty silver coins and gave them to him. This was a small amount of money; about the price of a common slave. It shows how little Judas was regarded by the chief priests.

Later, Matthew links this to the prophecy of Jeremiah (Matthew 27:9–10).

THE PASSOVER MEAL AND THE LAST SUPPER

MATTHEW 26:20–30

Every year Jews celebrate the Passover festival. It remembers the night the Israelites escaped from Egypt where they had been slaves (the Exodus). As Jesus was a Jew, he also celebrated the Passover every year. He had sent his disciples to make sure that everything was ready.

Jesus celebrated the Passover meal along with his disciples. Jesus suddenly announced that he would be betrayed by someone who was sitting at the table with him:

> *"One who dips his bread in the dish with me will betray me" (26:23).*

All of the disciples expressed shock and each of them asked Jesus if they had somehow done something to betray him. Judas asked, *"Surely not me?"*, but at this stage nobody knew who the traitor was because they had all dipped their bread in a common dish.

Jesus pointed out that the traitor would not escape God's judgement:

> *"It would have been better for that man if he had never been born"* (26:24).

What happened next has become the most important ritual for Christians everywhere. Jesus took elements of the Passover meal and made them symbols of his death.

Following the usual format of the Passover meal, Jesus blessed the bread, broke it, and passed it around. He did the same with the wine. Jesus explained that the bread was his body and that the wine was his blood, which sealed God's covenant. Just as the previous covenants between people and God had been sealed with sacrifice, Jesus' death would be the final sacrifice enabling all people to receive God's blessing and forgiveness:

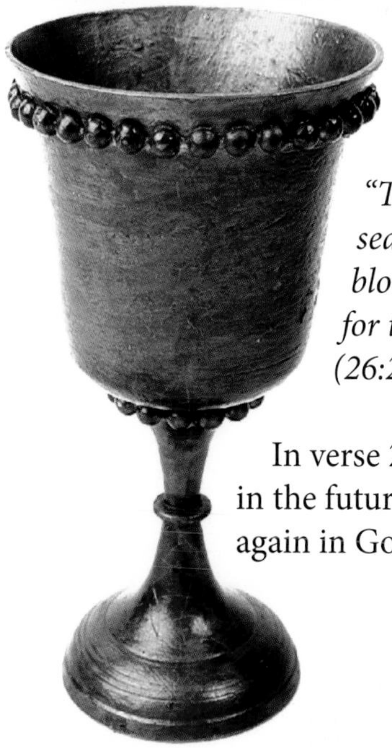

"This is my blood, which seals God's covenant, my blood poured out for many for the forgiveness of sins" (26:28).

In verse 29 Jesus refers to a time in the future when they would meet again in God's Kingdom.

At the Last Supper, Jesus used two of the items on the Passover table to symbolise his own forthcoming death. He took the unleavened bread and said *"this is my body"*. He also took the wine and said *"this is my blood"*. Christians today still remember that night by repeating the actions of eating bread and drinking wine. Different Christian traditions give this act of remembrance different names: Eucharist; Mass; The Lord's Supper; Holy Communion.

DIFFERENT UNDERSTANDINGS OF COMMUNION

Catholic Church

In the Catholic Church the Eucharist or Communion is celebrated daily in the **Mass**. Catholics believe that during the Eucharist the bread and wine change to become the body and blood of Christ. In other words, Christ becomes physically present in the bread and wine. This is known as **transubstantiation**.

Protestant tradition

In most Protestant churches, Communion is regarded as a memorial of Christ's death. The bread and wine do not change at all because they are simply symbols of what Christ has done. Communion means 'sharing' and at a Communion service Christians share together to remember the suffering and death of Christ.

NOTE

Passover

The Passover or *Seder* meal which Jesus had with his disciples followed a set format:

- An opening prayer and a blessing of the cup
- The dipping of herbs in salt water
- The breaking of unleavened bread
- The reading of the story of the Passover,
- The blessing of the second cup
- The festive meal of roast lamb
- The blessing of the third cup

Each item of food on the table symbolised what happened on the night of the first Passover when the Israelites escaped from Egypt. Jews today still celebrate the Passover.

FOR YOUR FOLDER

1. Describe the main events which took place during the Last Supper.
2. What new meaning did Jesus give to the bread and the wine?
3. Explain how communion is linked to the Passover meal.
4. Explain some differences in belief and practice for communion in Christian denominations today.

IN A GROUP

"The Christian Church places too much emphasis on the sacrament of communion and not enough on Christian behaviour".
Do you agree or disagree? Give reasons for your answer showing that you have considered different points of view.

THE EVENTS AT GETHSEMANE AND JESUS' ARREST

MATTHEW 26:20–30

The disciples went with Jesus to the Garden of Gethsemane, an olive tree plantation. His three closest disciples, Peter and the two sons of Zebedee (James and John), who had been with him at the Transfiguration, went further into the garden with him while he prayed. Jesus told them to 'watch and pray', and even though they probably realised that something momentous was about to happen, they were not able to stay awake.

Jesus uses the image of a 'cup of suffering' to symbolise the physical and spiritual suffering that he would experience. We see Jesus' humanity as he prays that the cup be taken away, yet he submits to God's will praying: *"Not what I want but what you want"* (26:39).

Jesus longed for his disciples to be close to him in his moments of distress as he thought about what lay ahead. He asked them three times to stay awake and keep watch, but they kept falling asleep. They did not appreciate the seriousness of what Jesus was going through. This meant that he had to cope with the mental suffering on his own.

The Significance of Gethsemane for Today

The events at the Garden of Gethsemane offer great comfort to Christians today when they are suffering things like bereavement or injustice. They believe that Jesus will understand what they are going through because he experienced so much suffering himself. Just like Jesus, Christians who suffer hand their problems over to God in prayer.

When Jesus prayed at Gethsemane he called God *abba*, which was a familiar term like 'daddy'. Many Christians feel that they can approach God like a loving father and talk to him about their problems.

Jesus knew that the time of his final suffering had come: *"The hour has come for the Son of Man to be handed over to the power of sinners"* (Matthew 26:45). Judas arrived with the Chief Priests and elders, and an armed crowd to arrest Jesus. In order to make sure the right man was arrested Judas kissed Jesus on the cheek, a common greeting in that culture, and said: *"Peace be with you, Teacher"* (26:49). He betrayed Jesus with an act of friendship. This makes Judas' betrayal even worse.

Jesus told Judas: *"Be quick about it friend"* (26:50). The rest of the disciples jumped to defend Jesus. One of those with Jesus drew his sword and cut off the ear of the High Priest's slave. Jesus told him to put his sword away and explained that the prophecies must come true. Jesus asked them why they had come to take him by surprise at night, as if he were an outlaw, saying that this also fulfiled prophecy.

The disciples were so afraid that they ran away.

IN A GROUP

Discuss the following questions:

1. **What can Christians learn from the behaviour of the disciples in this story?**
2. **Do you think this story can bring comfort to people in times of suffering?**
3. **Explain why Jesus submitted peacefully to his arrest. As the Messiah, what else could he have done?**
   As a revision task, look back to the story of Jesus' temptations (Matthew 4:1–11). Remind yourself of the powers that Jesus had.
4. **Can you think of any famous Christians whose faith has been tested? What happened and how did they overcome their time of testing?**

FOR YOUR FOLDER

1. **How did the disciples let Jesus down in Gethsemane?**
2. **What did Jesus mean when he said, "The hour has come"?**
3. **Pick out three phrases from Matthew 26:36–46 which describe Jesus' sorrow.**
4. **Why did Judas kiss Jesus?**
5. **Why do you think the disciples left Jesus when he was arrested?**
6. **Do you think it helps if people can talk to God in the same way they approach a loving father? Give reasons for your answer, showing that you have considered other viewpoints.**

JESUS BEFORE THE COUNCIL

MATTHEW 26:57–68

The Sanhedrin was the official Jewish council or court of justice. It had seventy one members, made up of Pharisees and Sadducees. The head of the council was the High Priest, who at the time of Jesus was Caiaphas.

The council was in control of the affairs of the Jewish people in Palestine. It had most of the powers of a normal court but was not allowed to carry out the death sentence. Only the Romans had the power to put someone to death.

Jesus was brought before the Sanhedrin on a charge of blasphemy, which means speaking in an offensive way about God. There were certain rules that had to be followed for a trial and it seems that Jesus' trial was carried out unfairly. For example:

- A court was not usually held in the High Priest's house. Jesus' trial took place in Caiaphas' house.
- Trials that could result in an execution could not take place at night. Jesus' trial was at night.
- False witnesses could be punished by death. At Jesus' trial two witnesses accused Jesus of threatening to destroy the Temple. (In John 2:19 Jesus told the Jewish authorities that if the Temple was torn down he would have the ability to rebuild it in three days. However, Jesus had not been talking about the real Temple but his body.)

At first Jesus did not answer this accusation, but when he was put under the oath and asked if he was the Messiah he replied: *"So you say"* (26:64). Jesus was careful not to agree with the High Priest's use of the word 'messiah', but went on to explain his identity in his own terms:

> *"You will see the Son of Man sitting on the right of the Almighty and coming on the clouds of heaven."*

You will remember that Son of Man is one of the titles that Jesus often used for himself. This time he makes reference to the prophecy of Daniel (Daniel 7:13).

The High Priest had heard enough and tore his robes to express his outrage at such blasphemy. Blasphemy was punishable by death by stoning according to the Jewish law (Leviticus 24:16). The others attacked Jesus, spitting, punching and mocking him.

FOR YOUR FOLDER

1. **What was the Sanhedrin?**
2. **Where was Jesus taken when he was arrested?**
3. **Explain the meaning of the term 'blasphemy'.**
4. **What accusation was brought against Jesus about the Temple?**
5. **Do you think Jesus was right to remain silent when questioned?**
6. **Why could the Sanhedrin not put Jesus to death?**

JESUS BEFORE PILATE

MATTHEW 27:1–2, 11-26

Pilate, the Roman Governor, was the only one who could officially sentence Jesus to death so the Jewish leaders handed him over for a second trial. The charge of blasphemy was twisted into a political charge because blasphemy was not a crime under Roman law. By saying that Jesus claimed to be the Messiah the Jewish leaders could argue that he was guilty of leading a rebellion against the Roman Empire.

It is not certain where the trial took place but it may have been in the fortress of Antonia (see map of Jerusalem on page 48). Pilate's question to Jesus probably arose out of the Sanhedrin's report that Jesus had claimed to be the Messiah. When Jesus was brought before Pilate he asked him: *"Are you the King of the Jews?"* (27:11). If Jesus was claiming to be a king it could be argued that he wanted to rule Palestine and overthrow the Romans.

Jesus did not say anything, which surprised Pilate and gave him no real reason to charge him. Pilate realised that Jesus was a threat to the authority of the Sanhedrin, and they were trying to get rid of him. He was also aware that Jesus was very popular among the ordinary people.

Pilate was clearly uneasy about the case against Jesus and this was confirmed by his wife as a result of a dream. Messages given in dreams were taken very seriously by the Romans. She told Pilate to *"have nothing to do with that innocent man"* (27:19). Matthew may have included this conversation in his account because it highlights Jesus' innocence.

In an attempt to find a simple solution, Pilate took the opportunity to use a Passover tradition. Every year the governor could set free one prisoner as a favour to the Jews. At the time there was a well known prisoner called Barabbas who had caused riots and was known to be a dangerous man. Pilate offered the crowd the choice of releasing either Jesus or Barabbas. It seemed obvious that the crowd would ask for Jesus to be released.

Pilate's plan backfired because the Sanhedrin persuaded the crowd to ask for Barabbas, a possible Zealot, to be released instead of Jesus. Clearly Pilate was frustrated at this and decided to wash his hands of any responsibility for the life of Jesus:

> *"I am not responsible for the death of this man! This is your doing!"*(27:24).

He must have felt very uneasy at sentencing a man to death with no real evidence. Washing one's hands to symbolise innocence was a Jewish custom (Deuteronomy 21:6; Psalm 26:6).

The crowd, so different now from the one that had welcomed Jesus into Jerusalem on Palm Sunday, shouted: *"Let the responsibility for his death fall on us and on our children!" (27:25).*

Pilate's job was to maintain Roman rule in Palestine, and that meant keeping good relations with the local leaders. Pilate did what the crowd wanted and sent Jesus to be crucified.

FOR YOUR FOLDER

1. **Describe the main features of Jesus' trial before Pilate**
2. **Explain why Pilate may have had doubts about Jesus' guilt.**
3. **Why did Pilate wash his hands at Jesus' trial?**
4. **What can Christians learn from the suffering and behaviour of Jesus at his trials?**

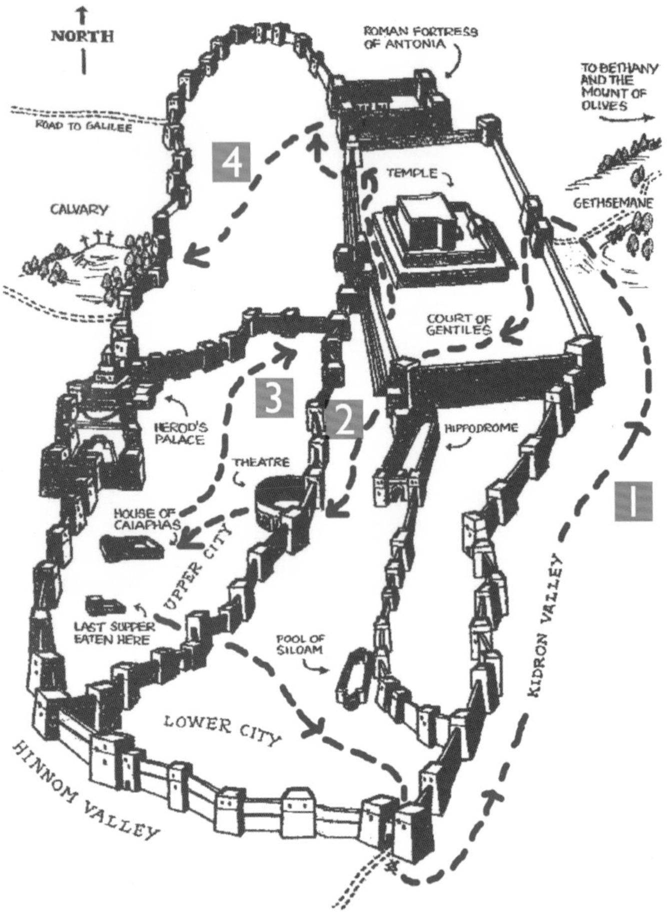

Use the references below and the map above to follow Jesus' movements through Jerusalem before his death.

Matthew 26 v30

Matthew 26 v57

Matthew 27 v1-2, v27-31

Matthew 27 v33

THE CRUCIFIXION AND DEATH OF JESUS

MATTHEW 27:32-61

Crucifixions took place outside the city wall on a hill called *Golgotha*– 'the place of the skull'. Crucifixion was the most extreme form of Roman execution, reserved for the worst criminals. Jewish scripture described anyone who died by crucifixion as *"under God's curse"* (Deuteronomy 21:22–23). The place of Jesus' death symbolised rejection by people and by God.

Golgotha: Can you see why it is called the place of the skull?

At that time it was not unusual to make a prisoner carry the cross-beam of their own cross to the site of the crucifixion. The fact that Jesus needed the assistance of a man from Cyrene to carry his cross probably shows that he was weak from the torture and beating he had received from the Roman soldiers (27:27–31).

The soldiers offered Jesus a drink – a kind of painkiller, which he refused. He was crucified between two criminals. The charge against each criminal would have been written at the top of their cross. In Jesus' case it would have read *IESUS NAZAREUS REX IUDAEORUM* – 'Jesus of Nazareth, King of the Jews' .

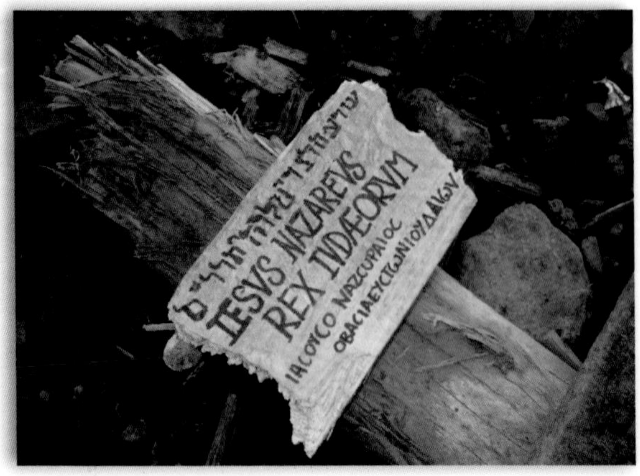

The Romans crucified people publicly as an example to others. Matthew records that people gathered to watch and even shouted abuse at those condemned. The crowd laughed at Jesus' weakness and reminded him of his claims to have the power of God.

The prophet Isaiah describes the Messiah as a suffering servant:

"He was arrested and led off to die, and no one cared about his fate. He was put to death for the sins of our people" (Isaiah 53:8).

Matthew here presents Jesus as that suffering servant, forsaken and rejected by everyone and yet at the same time, fulfilling the prophecies about the Messiah.

FOR YOUR FOLDER

Complete the phrases Jesus was mocked with:

1. **"You were going to tear down the Temple and build it up in three days…"**
2. **"He saved others, but he cannot save himself! Isn't he the king of Israel?..."**
3. **"He trusts in God and claims to be God's Son…"**

Matthew records some strange and amazing things that happened during the last hours of Jesus' life. The whole region was covered in darkness, even though it was the middle of the day. In the Jewish scriptures darkness was often a symbol of tragedy or judgement (Exodus10:21–23; Amos 8:9–10).

Jesus then called out the words of Psalm 22:1: *"Eli Eli, lema sabacthani"* which means "My God, my God, why did you abandon me?" Some people thought he was calling for the prophet Elijah who, it was believed, would help those in need.

After Jesus had cried out and died there was an earthquake; people rose from the dead and the curtain hanging in the Holy of Holies was torn in two, from top to bottom. Both are symbolic events:

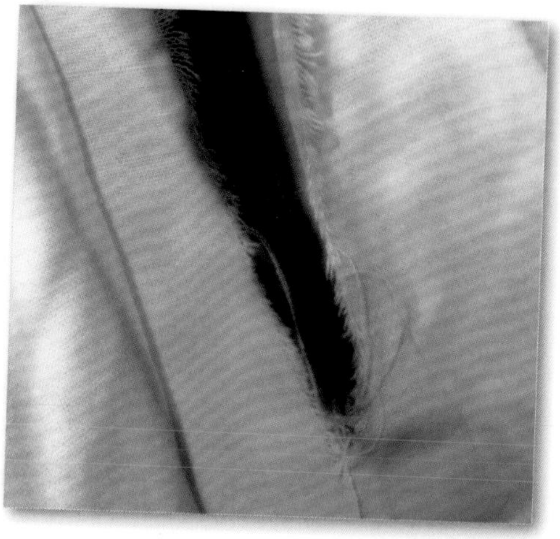

The Holy of Holies was the part of the Temple where the presence of God was said to dwell (see page 16). It was separated from the rest of the temple by a thick curtain. Strict instructions were given concerning the location of this curtain:

"Make a curtain of fine linen woven with blue, purple and red wool. Embroider it with figures of winged creatures. Hang it on four posts of acacia wood covered with gold, fitted with hooks, and set in four silver bases…The curtain will separate the Holy Place from the Most Holy Place" (Exodus 26:31–33).

Only the High Priest could pass through the curtain into God's presence, once a year, having performed complex rituals in preparation.

If the curtain had been torn by human hands the tear would have begun at the bottom. Matthew records that the curtain was torn from *"top to bottom"* (27:51) which suggests that God himself tore the curtain. The destruction of the curtain, which symbolically separated people from God, represented that the way to God was now open. All people could now come before God.

The dead being raised to life represented the future for all those who trusted in Christ's death as a sacrifice which would bring them forgiveness.

It was only after Jesus had died that the soldiers realised that he really was the 'Son of God' (27:54) The darkness, earthquake and other supernatural events probably convinced them that this was no ordinary execution.

Matthew draws attention to the presence of the women who watched the crucifixion from a distance (27:55–56). They did not run away like the disciples. These same women stayed at the cross and were the first at the tomb (28:1), which shows how devoted they were to Jesus. Matthew even identifies them by name (27:56).

A rich man from Arimathea, called Joseph, asked Pilate for the body of Jesus so that he could bury him in his own tomb. Corpses from crucifixions were usually burned at the town dump, so Joseph obviously would have risked his own life by approaching Pilate with such a request. This shows the love and respect he had for Jesus.

The tomb was sealed by a stone and a guard was placed beside it to make sure that the disciples did not steal the body and pretend that Jesus has been resurrected. The two Marys also sat close by and watched.

FOR YOUR FOLDER

1. **Why would the events of the last week of Jesus' life have been a difficult time for the disciples?**
2. **Jesus was crucified at Golgotha. What is the meaning of 'Golgotha'?**
3. **What part did Simon of Cyrene play in the events leading up to the crucifixion?**
3. **Describe three of the supernatural events that Matthew recorded when Jesus died.**
4. **What was Jesus saying when he cried out *"Eli, Eli, lema sabacthani"*?**
5. **What did the Roman soldier say after Jesus' death?**
6. **Why is the death of Jesus important for Christians?**
7. **If Jesus was a good man, and the 'Son of God' why was he put to death?**

IN A GROUP

1. **Who was responsible for the Death of Jesus?**

Traditionally the Jewish leaders have been blamed for the death of Jesus. The Gospels stress the part they played, even though the final decision was made by the Romans. Other people also played significant roles in the events leading up to Jesus' death.

Look at the following list of people and write a sentence on the part they played in the death of Jesus:

The disciples	Herod
Judas	Pilate
The Jewish leaders	The crowd
	Jesus himself
Caiaphas	God

Write a paragraph on who you think was most responsible for the death of Jesus.

2. **"Save yourself if you are God's Son."**

Do you think Jesus should have avoided crucifixion? Discuss in small groups.

JESUS' RESURRECTION

MATTHEW 28:1-10

Early on the Sunday morning the two Marys, Mary Magdalene and Mary, mother of James and Joseph (27:56), returned to the tomb.

More strange events took place when they arrived; there was another earthquake and an angel appeared, rolled away the stone from the entrance to Jesus' tomb, and sat on it. Matthew explains that the soldiers were so frightened that they became *"like dead men"* (28:4), which probably means that they either fainted from shock or were knocked out during the earthquake.

The angel then spoke directly to the women with amazing news that Jesus had been raised from the dead, just as he said he would be (see 16:21; 17:23; 20:18–19). For further proof the angel pointed to the empty tomb where Jesus' body should have been. Excited, the women ran to tell the disciples what had happened, but before they got there they met Jesus himself and fell at his feet in worship. His sudden appearance probably shocked them. Jesus told them to tell his disciples what had happened and said he would meet them in Galilee.

FOR YOUR FOLDER

1. **What did the women see and experience when they returned to the tomb on the Sunday morning?**
2. **Explain the significance of Jesus' appearance to the women.**
3. **What would the resurrection have meant to the disciples?**
4. **Explain why belief in the resurrection is an essential part of the Christian faith.**

IN A GROUP

"The importance of Jesus' death and resurrection for Christians cannot be underestimated. The two events go hand-in-hand and are the basis of the Christian faith."

1. **Look at the following reasons given and place them in order, starting with the reason that you think is most important:**

- **Jesus' death and resurrection shows that God can defeat the powers of evil, even death itself.**
- **Jesus' death and resurrection prove that Jesus was who he claimed to be; the promised Messiah.**
- **Jesus' crucifixion changed the way people relate to God. The way is now open between people and God.**
- **The resurrection shows that there is life after death. This gives hope of everlasting life. Christians believe that they, too, will have life after death.**
- **Jesus paid the price for people's sin.**

2. **Do you think that Jesus' death is more important for Christians today than his resurrection?**

CLASS DEBATE: Did the Resurrection really happen?

'Belief in the physical resurrection of Jesus is difficult in the twenty-first century.'
Do you agree or disagree? Give reasons for your answer.

Most Christians accept that the resurrection of Jesus was a real event. However, there is an ongoing debate about whether or not the resurrection really happened or if it was just a symbolic event. In groups discuss the following theories that have been put forward. See if you can fill in any information in the missing boxes.

ARGUMENTS AGAINST	ARGUMENTS FOR
Jesus did not die but was only unconscious. The coolness of the tomb helped him revive and he got out of it with the help of the disciples.	If this was true then what happened to Jesus?
Jesus did die but the disciples stole the body and then made up the story of the resurrection to convince people that Jesus was alive.	After the resurrection the disciples were prepared to risk everything for their faith. This is hard to believe if the resurrection had just been a trick.
Jesus did die but the followers of Jesus, in their distress, hallucinated because they wanted to believe that Jesus had risen.	The authorities were not able to produce the body to prove them wrong.
The women failed to see the body of Jesus at the tomb because they went to the wrong tomb.	

IN A GROUP

Discuss:

Does it matter whether the resurrection of Jesus really happened or not?

Would it be enough for Jesus to live on through his teachings? Consider 1 Corinthians 15.12–19.

Chapter 6

THE PLACE AND NATURE OF CHRISTIAN DISCIPLESHIP

All rabbis or teachers in Jesus' day had disciples who learned from their teaching and tried to follow in their footsteps. Jesus was no exception. He had twelve close followers or disciples who helped him in his ministry.

Jesus demanded total commitment from his disciples. Through his teaching he clearly stated that God should be first in their lives, above everything else. In the examples we will be studying it is clear that Jesus' disciples had a lot to learn and at times they had great difficulty in understanding what they were being taught. Christians today also see themselves as disciples of Jesus and try to live as closely as possible to his teaching.

Discipleship

A disciple is a follower or a learner. For example, in the world of work, a person might be a trainee mechanic who learns his trade from a fully qualified mechanic. This is called an apprenticeship.

Jesus' disciples made sacrifices to follow him. To be a Christian today also requires sacrifice. Some of the sacrifices a person might have to make in committing to Christianity include the following:

Attitudes towards money and possessions
"Can you have a lot of money and be a Christian?"

Service to others
"What should I do to help others?"

Friendships
"Who am I spending my time with?'

Priorities
"What are the most important things in my life?"

Popularity
"Am I prepared to give up my popularity?"

Comfortable lifestyle
"I have a great lifestyle. I'm not prepared to make any changes to follow Christ."

FURTHER THINKING

What sacrifices might someone have to make if they followed Christ?

JESUS CALLS HIS DISCIPLES

JESUS CALLS SIMON AND ANDREW

MATTHEW 4:18-20

Simon and his brother Andrew were fishermen. When Jesus said to them *"follow me"* (4:19), he was asking them to leave their jobs. Matthew is interested in how these men responded to the call. Notice that they dropped everything to follow Jesus, and that they responded immediately. Jesus told them that he would make them *"fishers of men"* (4:19). This meant that he would teach them how to spread the Christian faith. Simon was later given the nickname *Peter* by Jesus, which means 'rock'. He was to become one of Jesus' closest disciples.

JESUS CALLS MATHEW

MATTHEW 9:9–13

Matthew was a tax collector. Remember that tax collectors were hated because they were dishonest and worked for the Romans (see page 13). Jesus' actions here would have horrified the Jewish religious leaders. As far as they were concerned Matthew was a sinner and an outcast. Yet Jesus called him to be one of his disciples. Like Simon and Andrew, Matthew responded immediately to the call of Jesus.

It seems that a celebration followed in the form of a meal at Matthew's house. Friends of Matthew's, also tax collectors, were also present. This angered the Jewish religious leaders. According to Jewish law, a Jew could not associate with outcasts like tax collectors as they were considered 'unclean'. This did not mean physical dirtiness, but religious impurity. By eating with such people Jesus was in danger of breaking the ritual laws.

The Pharisees asked Jesus *"Why do you eat with tax collectors and other outcasts?"* (9:11). Jesus' reply showed that, unlike most religious teachers, he was more concerned with helping the outcasts in society than keeping religious duties. To help everyone to understand this, Jesus used an everyday example – doctors are not needed for those who are in good health, but for the sick.

FOR YOUR FOLDER

1. Name two disciples who were brothers.
2. Which disciple was a tax collector?
3. Why did Jesus make friends with outcasts and sinners?
4. 'Christians should be prepared to mix with all kinds of people.' Do you agree or disagree?

FURTHER THINKING

Jesus did not go to these people because they received him warmly but because they needed him. How could this apply today?

How are Christians called to carry out God's work today?

Two people describe how they were led to carry out God's work:

Steve Stockman is a Presbyterian minister, who is chaplain at Queen's University Belfast. Steve is also a regular contributor to BBC Radio Ulster and author of **'Walk On; The Spiritual Journey of U2'** which is now translated into seven languages!

Steve talks about what he thinks it means to be called by God in the twenty-first century:

"I believe that first of all I am called by God to be 'me'. As a Christian it is important to discover your calling in life, so that you can help bring about God's Kingdom here on Earth. Your role is just as important whether you are called to work behind the till at your local supermarket or called to be a minister. Every Christian is called to be a witness to Christ.

"Frederick Buechner, who is a Presbyterian minister and novelist, says that vocation (calling) should be 'where your deepest gladness meets the world's greatest need.'

"I believe I was given the gift of communication. This is what drew me to become a Presbyterian minister. It is no more important than other vocations but it is where my deepest gladness meets the world's deepest need.

"I believe that through prayer and talking to others you can find out what God is calling you to do with your life. Then, by doing and getting on with it, if you experience a sense of fulfillment and deep gladness, you will know you are in the right place."

Father John is the parish priest in a small country Catholic parish:

"I came to an awareness of vocation (call) on three levels: creative, emotional and spiritual. However, it wasn't until I left school that I made the decision that I might become a priest. The seeds were sown years before.

"I had been in the Cathedral Choir and it was there that I developed a love of music – all sorts really, from Pop music to Classical. I really liked the music of the 'old' church. For a long time I couldn't decide between a career as a musician or as a priest. I found out that I could combine the two as a priest with a ministry in music. I use music as a way to reach out to people.

"The desire to become a priest was even deeper on the emotional and spiritual levels. I came from what would now be called a 'dysfunctional' family. Alcoholism was the problem. During my teenage years this really upset me. I received a lot of help and support from the priests at my boarding school. They were the only people I could turn to for advice and guidance. The memory of that stayed with me all these years and I think it was through their openness and influence that I have been able to help people in similar situations."

IN A GROUP

Explain how Steve and Father John were influenced to take up full time Christian work.

Make a list of the type of work that each of them might carry out as part of their ministry.

THE SERMON ON THE MOUNT

Jesus' teaching in Matthew Chapter 5–7 is known as **The Sermon on the Mount**. Just as Moses received the Ten Commandments on a mountain, Matthew shows Jesus on a mountain, teaching on their true meaning. God's covenant with Moses is compared with the New Covenant.

Jesus believed that the outward keeping of the law was not enough to please God. Instead he stresses the importance of a person's attitude, as well as a person's actions. Jesus gave six examples of Jewish teaching given by Moses and explained what he thought they meant. In this section we will look at three of these examples: Jesus' teaching on anger, revenge and love of enemies.

Anger

MATTHEW 5:21–26

Jesus took one of the Ten Commandments and took its meaning further. The sixth commandment says: *"Do not commit murder, anyone who does will be brought to trial"* (5:21). Jesus explained that there is a much deeper meaning to this commandment. The command not to murder is not just concerned with the final act of murder but the negative emotions that can lead to someone committing murder.

If people get angry they should not allow their anger to continue or fester.
Jesus teaches that having good relationships with each other is more important than religious services: If a person is about to make sacrifice at the temple, but realises they have an ongoing argument with someone, they should leave their sacrifice and go and make peace.

Linked to this is also the issue of 'name-calling'. Jesus taught that a person who insults others by their words is in danger of going to hell.

Revenge

MATTHEW 5:38–42

Seeking revenge was acceptable under the Old Covenant. The law of retaliation said: *"An eye for an eye and a tooth for a tooth"* (Exodus 21:24). The purpose of this was to limit revenge. So if someone knocked out your tooth, you could knock out their tooth and nothing more. By the time of Jesus this was no longer taken literally, however money was used instead. So if someone wronged you, then you were entitled to sue them.

Jesus taught that all revenge is wrong. He taught his followers that they should 'turn the other cheek', even if severely provoked by someone. In practice this meant being good, even to people who treat you badly. Jesus may have been teaching his followers to shame those who wronged them into doing the right thing.

FOR YOUR FOLDER

Complete Jesus' instructions to his followers regarding revenge:

1. **If someone slaps you on the right cheek…**
2. **If someone takes you to court to sue you for your shirt…**
3. **If one of the occupation troops forces you to carry his pack one kilometre…**

Love for enemies

MATTHEW 5:42–48

The command to *"love your neighbour as you love yourself"* comes from Leviticus 19:18. Over time it had turned into a saying, 'Love your neighbour and hate your enemies'. However, the phrase 'and hate your enemies' is not found in scripture. The people had interpreted this to mean that they should love fellow Jews but that they ought to hate their enemies.

Jesus told his followers to *"love your enemies and pray for those who persecute you"* (5:44). There is nothing particularly difficult about loving your friends. In fact, that is easy to do (see 5:47). Loving enemies was a radical new idea that would have shocked Jesus' listeners. How could they love or pray for the Romans who occupied their land and often treated them badly?

Martin Luther King attempted to put Jesus' teachings from the Sermon on the Mount into practice in his own life. He led the American Civil Rights campaign during the 1960s, which tried to achieve equality for black Americans.

Although his protest brought him into confrontation with the authorities he always insisted that his followers acted in a non-violent way. They participated in forms of protest such as sit-ins or mass meetings which people couldn't ignore but which weren't violent. Martin Luther King's turn-the-other-cheek policy represented the best way to make his point; to expose the brutality of his opponents and to create a positive, harmonious future.

"Love even for enemies is the key to the solution of the problems of our world – Jesus is not an impractical idealist; he is the practical realist."

"Darkness cannot drive out darkness; only light can do that. Hate cannot drive out hate; only love can do that. Hate multiplies hate, violence multiplies violence and toughness multiplies toughness ... so when Jesus says 'Love your enemies,' he is setting forth a profound and ultimately inescapable admonition."

'Strength to Love' – Martin Luther King
(Hodder & Stoughton, 1964.)

IN A GROUP

1. Do you think that Jesus' teaching on non-violence is a practical guide for Christian behaviour today?
2. *"How you live is more important than what you believe."*
   Do you agree? Give reasons for your opinion.

FURTHER THINKING

1. Do you think people put Jesus teaching to 'love your enemies' into practice?
2. What would happen if soldiers in a warzone started following Jesus' teaching to love their enemies?

FOR YOUR FOLDER

Complete the following table comparing the Old Covenant with Jesus' teaching on the New Covenant:

	ANGER	REVENGE	LOVE FOR ENEMIES
Old Covenant	"Do not commit murder. Anyone who does will be brought to trial."		
New Covenant		"Do not take revenge on someone who wrongs you...	

THE DEMANDS OF DISCIPLESHIP

Salt and Light

MATTHEW 5:13–16

Jesus used an everyday item to explain the demands of discipleship. He taught that his followers should be like salt.

Salt has two functions: It can bring out the flavour of the food it is put on, and it is used as a preservative to stop meat from decaying. Only a small amount of salt can be very effective. However, if salt loses its flavour then it is useless. If you look through your kitchen cupboard at home you may find some jars of spices that are out of date. They will not flavour a dish as well as fresh spices. Jesus teaches that Christians who have lost their commitment to God, or their distinctiveness, will have no effect on the world around them.

Jesus reinforced this teaching by using another example. He said that Christians should be like light. He used the example of a city on a hill. Unless the city is lit up it cannot be seen at night. In the same way it makes no sense to hide a light under a bowl. Jesus meant that his followers' faith must shine out in the world as an example to others.

If Christians did not set a good example then they would be as ineffective as a light that is hidden under a bowl.

Christians today can show their faith in a number of different ways. They can be fair and kind; take a moral stand on issues such as injustice, violence, discrimination and poverty. True Christianity is not just about words of belief. It calls for a practical faith.

Counting the Cost

MATTHEW 16:24–26

This teaching highlights the extent of the commitment Jesus expected from his followers. Being a true disciple of Jesus would require self-denial. Committed Christians must be willing to face even death for the sake of the Gospel:

> *"If any of you want to come with me, you must forget yourself, carry your cross, and follow me."* (16:24)

It was a Roman custom for a person facing crucifixion to carry part of their own cross. It publicly showed the person submitting to the rule he had opposed. In the same way Christians had to publicly show that they submitted to Christ's authority.

In the first three centuries AD many Christians in the Roman Empire were martyred for their belief in Christ. This means that they were put to death. For example, it is believed that the apostle Peter was crucified upside down for his faith.

The suffering endured by these Christians is an example of how some people were prepared to 'carry their cross'. In other words they knew they might die for their faith but still they remained faithful to Christ. Some Christians today also face the possibility of death for their faith; others may simply suffer mockery or loss of friends. Either way, to be a Christian usually involves some sort of sacrifice.

FOR YOUR FOLDER

1. Jesus said *"If any of you want to come with me, you must forget yourself, carry your cross, and follow me."* Give two examples of how a Christian may be asked to do this.
2. What do you think is the most effective way for Christians to be like salt and light?.
3. What do you think is most difficult about the Christian way of life?
4. Do you think it is more difficult to be a Christian today than in the time of the first disciples?

RELIGIOUS OBSERVANCES

Teaching about charity

MATTHEW 6:1–4

How important is money to you? Do you have a part-time job? Do you get money for babysitting or doing chores around the house? Are you lucky enough to get pocket money? Look at the following pie-chart. Draw a similar one using the pupils in your class to show how your class spends money. Some suggestions are:

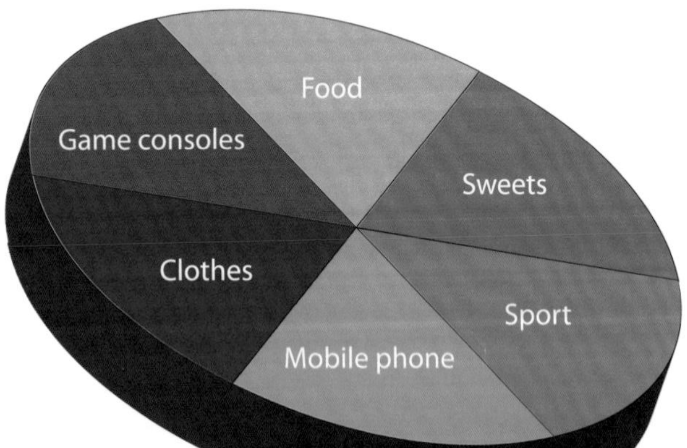

At the time of Jesus religious duties involved charity, prayer and fasting. Jesus taught that those who carry out these duties to gain a good reputation get exactly that – but nothing more. He pointed out that *"they have already been paid in full"* (6:2). Jesus called such people hypocrites. Religious people were giving money to charity which is a kind and humble thing to do, yet they were proud and boastful about the way that they did it. Instead Jesus taught that Christians should give to the needy in such a way that only God knows about it. Then they would be rewarded appropriately.

Look back at the pie-chart you made in your class. Did anyone consider giving to charity as part of it? Christians believe that giving to charity is very important, no matter how much money you have. There are many ways to give privately to charity. Can you make a list?

RED NOSE DAY

Red Nose Day is a UK-wide fundraising event organised by Comic Relief every two years. On Red Nose Day everyone is encouraged to cast inhibitions aside, put on a Red Nose and do something a little bit silly to raise money - celebrities included! It culminates in a night of extraordinary comedy and moving documentary films on BBC One.

It's an event that unites the entire nation in trying to make a difference to the lives of thousands of people, both across Africa and in the UK, who face terrible injustice or who live in abject poverty.

Find out more at **www.rednoseday.com**

Prayer

MATTHEW 6:5–8

FOR YOUR FOLDER

Make a list of occasions when people pray.

Do you pray? Can you think of a time when praying helped you?

Jesus began his teaching on prayer by saying how not to pray:

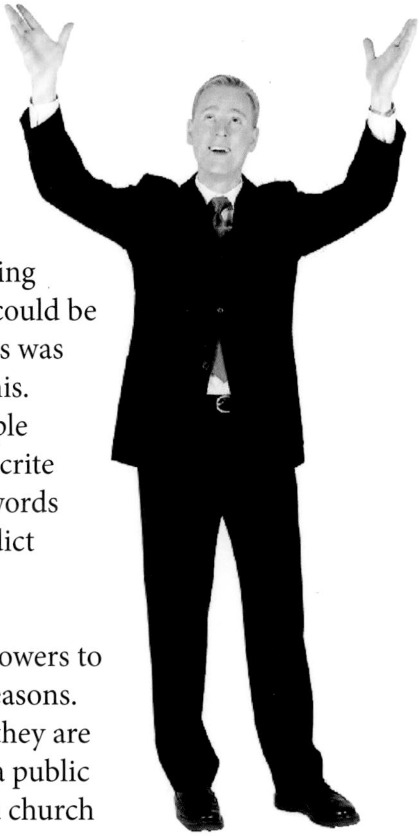

Don't show off – Synagogues were places of worship where Jews gathered to pray. It was not unusual to hear people praying loudly just so they could be seen by others. Jesus was not impressed by this. He called such people **hypocrites**. A hypocrite is a person whose words and actions contradict each other.

Jesus taught his followers to pray for the right reasons. It doesn't matter if they are on their own or in a public gathering, such as a church service. They are not praying simply to be seen and praised by others.

Don't use a lot of meaningless words – The Gentiles' prayers were long because they thought that this practice would impress their many gods. Jesus taught that his followers did not need to be like that because God knows what they need before they ask.

Types of Prayer

Prayer can take many forms. The following examples are a way that prayer can be divided into different types:

Praise/adoration A prayer in which Christians show adoration to God

Confession A prayer in which Christians confess they have sinned and ask for forgiveness

Thanksgiving A prayer in which Christians thank God for what he has done in their lives

Petition A prayer in which Christians ask God for what they need in their lives

Intercession A prayer in which Christians ask God for what other people need in their lives

The Lord's Prayer

MATTHEW 6:9–15

The Lord's Prayer or 'Our Father' is one of the most well known Christian prayers. It has always been very important to the Christian Church and is still recited today in churches, schools and Christian gatherings throughout the world. It unites people all over the world in their faith and gives them a common focus, regardless of which Christian tradition they follow.

The prayer was given by Jesus to his disciples and it sums up Jesus' teaching about the Kingdom of God. In the prayer we can see different types of prayer, such as praise, confession, thanksgiving, petition and intercession.

The Lord's Prayer	Reference	Meaning	Type of Prayer
"Our Father in Heaven"	6:9	Jesus used the word *abba* which means 'daddy' when he prayed to God This teaches that God wants the best for his children and is as approachable as a loving father. There is also reverence and awe in approaching God.	Praise
"May your holy name be honoured"	6:9	This highlights the importance of putting God's glory first before personal needs are prayed for.	Praise
"May your kingdom come, may your will be done on earth as it is in heaven"	6:10	The Bible teaches that when Jesus came to earth as a man, God's kingdom also arrived. Through these words Jesus urges his followers to pray for God's will to be carried out on earth.	Intercession
"Give us today the food we need."	6:11	People do not just need physical food to be well. They also have emotional and spiritual needs. These words imply that God will supply this help each day as it is needed.	Petition
"Forgive us the wrongs we have done, as we forgive the wrongs that others have done to us."	6:12	Jesus reminded his followers that only those who were prepared to forgive could ask for forgiveness. This is an important part of being a Christian.	Confession
"Do not bring us to hard testing, but deliver us from the evil one."	6:13	These words are usually translated as 'lead us not into temptation.' It is a request that Jesus' followers will be able to resist any temptations that they may face. 'The evil one' is another name for the devil .	Petition
Many Greek manuscripts add the words: *"For yours is the kingdom the power and the glory, forever and ever. Amen."*		This is further acknowledgement of the wonder and awe of God and his power.	Praise
Comment on forgiveness	6:14–15	At the end of the prayer Jesus reinforced the idea that God's forgiveness is dependant upon his followers' readiness to forgive others.	

FURTHER THINKING

1. "Prayer is a waste of time. If God has everyone's life planned out anyway what is the point?" Discuss this statement in a small group.

2. Do you think that daily repetition of prayers like the Lord's Prayer makes prayer meaningless?

Fasting

MATTHEW 6:16–18

For Jews, fasting meant going without food to take part in an activity like prayer with greater concentration. Prayers of confession and petition were often accompanied by fasting. Some Jews fasted regularly, for example, the Pharisees fasted twice a week (Luke 18:12). However, Jesus criticised the actions of people who fasted only to gain the admiration of others. Again Jesus said that since that is all they wanted, that is all they would get.

Jesus did not want to discourage his followers from fasting, but he taught that people should try to look as normal as possible when they fast and not draw attention to themselves by looking hungry or miserable. Only God should know what they are doing. Jesus assured them that God would reward them.

FOR YOUR FOLDER

1. Name two places where the hypocrites liked to pray or give to the needy.
2. Why did the hypocrites like to make a public display of praying and giving to the needy?
4. How might Jesus' teaching on prayer have upset some of his Jewish listeners?
5. Do you think it should matter whether we give in secret or in public when supporting a charity?

FORGIVENESS

As well as teaching about forgiveness through the Lord's Prayer, Jesus gave practical guidelines and clear examples of how he expected his followers to act in a forgiving way.

The Parable of the Unforgiving Servant

MATTHEW 18:21–35

This parable is told in answer to a question about forgiveness. Peter asked Jesus:

> *"Lord, if my brother keeps on sinning against me, how many times do I have to forgive him? Seven?"* (18:21)

In Jewish tradition the number seven was a symbol for completeness or perfection. So to forgive seven times would be a gracious act. However, Jesus' reply stressed that forgiveness has no limits:

> *"No, not seven times but seventy times seven."* (18:22)

Jesus then went on to explain his answer through a parable: A servant owed a king 'millions of pounds' which he knew he could never repay even if he was sold as a slave, along with his wife and family. The servant went to the king and promised the impossible: to repay the king everything.

The king felt sorry for him because he knew that this was impossible, and so he cancelled the debt. The fact that the debt was so big shows the extent of the king's forgiveness.

However, the forgiven servant quickly forgot how forgiving the king had been. When the servant met a fellow servant who could not repay a debt he refused to be patient with him and threw him into jail. The first servant failed to learn from the king's example. When the king heard this he was outraged and immediately withdrew his forgiveness from the unforgiving servant. He put the first servant into jail until he paid back his own debt.

The parable means that because Christians have been forgiven so much themselves, then they must never be unwilling to forgive others.

FOR YOUR FOLDER

1. How many times did Peter think a person should be forgiven?
2. How many times did Jesus say a person should be forgiven?
3. Retell the parable of the Unforgiving Servant in your own words.
4. "A Christian should always forgive no matter what the situation." Do you agree or disagree? Give reasons for your answer showing you have considered different points of view.

IN A GROUP

Look in newspaper and magazine articles for crimes against people. Group stories into those you could easily forgive and those that you would have difficulty in forgiving.

Look at the group of stories where you think forgiveness is difficult and discuss the following questions:

- What effects does not forgiving have on communities of people?
- Why is it important for communities to try to live in harmony (community cohesion)?
- Is Jesus' teaching on forgiveness practical for community cohesion?

FURTHER THINKING

Find out what you can about Gordon Wilson. His daughter, Marie, was one of eleven people killed in an IRA bomb in Enniskillen in 1987.

JESUS CHALLENGES A MAN'S ATTITUDE TO WEALTH

MATTHEW 19:16-26

IN A GROUP

What do you think it would be like to win the lottery? Would you tell people? What would you do with the money? Would you still live in the same house or town? Would you give money to your friends? Who would you give money to? How much would you give away? Where would you draw the line? Think about how your life would change. Would you be happier than you are now?

A man came to Jesus because he wanted to know what good thing he should do to receive eternal life. Jesus told him to keep the Commandments and he listed some as examples: do not murder; do not steal; do not accuse anyone falsely; respect your father and mother; and love your neighbour as you love yourself. The man told Jesus that he had obeyed all the commandments. Jesus then told him the final step he could take if he wanted to be 'perfect' was to:

> *"...go and sell all you have and give the money to the poor, and you will have riches in heaven" (v21).*

Imagine how the man felt! He obviously had a lot of money and possessions. The fact that he went away sad suggests that he wanted to follow Jesus but was unwilling to give up his wealth.

Jesus placed great importance on a person's attitude to money. He went on to tell his disciples:

> *"I assure you: it will be very hard for rich people to enter the Kingdom of heaven. I repeat: it is much harder for a rich person to enter the kingdom of God than for a camel to go through the eye of a needle"(19:23–24).*

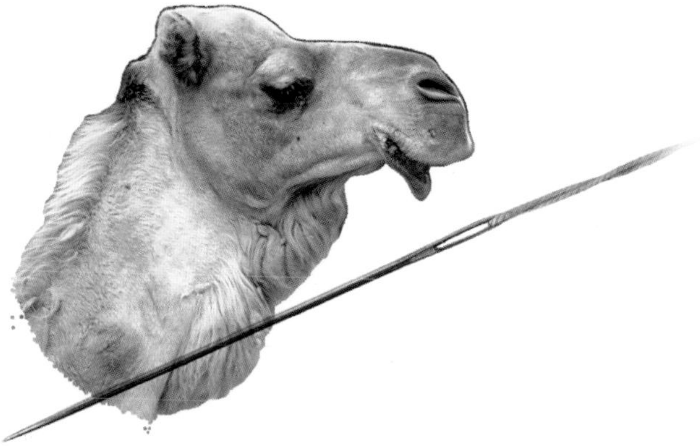

Jesus uses this figure of speech to emphasise his point– it is almost impossible for the rich to enter the Kingdom of God (The saying 'eye of the needle' could refer to a small door in the city wall. The door was only large enough for a person, and a camel would never be able to fit through).

The disciples would have been stunned by this teaching. The people of this time looked upon riches as a blessing from God or a reward for good behaviour. The rich were always considered to have been favoured by God. If this was not the case then it seemed as if no one could be saved.

FOR YOUR FOLDER

1. **Name two things the man had to do to receive eternal life.**
2. **Why did the young man go away sad?**
3. **What comparison did Jesus make to show how difficult it would be for a rich person to enter the Kingdom of Heaven?**
4. **Why would the disciples have found it hard to accept the idea that riches could stand in the way of entry into the kingdom?**
5. **What lessons about money and possessions can be learned from the attitude and teaching of Jesus?**
7. **Do you think Jesus' teaching about money and possessions is relevant for Christians today?**

IN A GROUP

Some Christians take this passage literally and believe that they should give up any wealth to enter the Kingdom of God. Others argue that the story simply means that they must put God before any material things. Do you think you can be a Christian and also be rich?

THE PRESSURE OF DISCIPLESHIP

Jesus predicts Peter's denial

MATTHEW 26:31–35

One of the pressures of being a follower of Jesus comes in the form of peer pressure. It may be easy to say you are a Christian if everyone else around you believes the same thing, but it is a different matter if faced with someone who ridicules you for your faith. Some people might find that they want to keep their heads down and not admit their beliefs.

In this passage Jesus makes three predictions. Firstly, he explains how his followers will be scattered after he dies. Secondly, he predicts that he will rise again. This should have completely amazed the disciples but it seems they did not register its significance. Their attention is on his third prediction: that Peter will deny knowing Jesus three times:

> *"I tell you that before the cock crows tonight, you will say three times that you do not know me"* (26:34).

Peter confidently shrugs off the suggestion that he could be disloyal and says he will never deny that he is a follower of Jesus. He even argues that he would be prepared to die with Jesus and the rest of the disciples say they would face death too.

Peter denies Jesus

MATTHEW 26:69–74

It is not long before Jesus' prediction about Peter comes true. During Jesus' trial before the Sanhedrin Peter was waiting outside in a courtyard. He was approached by several people who suggested that they had seen him with Jesus. The first person who accused him was one of the High Priest's servant women. This was repeated by another servant woman. Finally a few men also accused him, arguing that his accent gave him away. But three times he denied it, as Jesus had predicted. It was only when he heard a cock crowing that he remembered what Jesus had said, and he went away feeling a deep sense of regret at denying that he knew Jesus.

FOR YOUR FOLDER

1. **What did Jesus say the disciples would do before the night was over?**
2. **What was Peter's response to the suggestion that he might deny Christ?**
3. **When Jesus was being tried before the Sanhedrin what happened to Peter as he waited outside?**
4. **Explain the significance of the cock crowing.**
5. **Why do you think Peter denied Christ?**
6. **What might tempt Christians today to deny Christ?**
7. **'The pressures facing Christians today are much more difficult than those faced by the first disciples.' Do you agree or disagree?**

THE GREAT COMMISSION

MATTHEW 28:16-20

After his death and resurrection, Jesus appeared to the disciples in Galilee and told them:

> *"Go, then, to all peoples everywhere and make them my disciples: baptise them in the name of the Father, the Son, and the Holy Spirit, and teach them to obey everything I have commanded you. And I will be with you always, to the end of the age"* (26:19–20).

This is called **The Great Commission**. Down through the ages Jesus' followers have obeyed the commission, and today there are people in all parts of the world who believe that they too should carry out the Great Commission. Many Christians become missionaries and spread the Gospel throughout the world. Others simply follow the commission at home by living a life that is pleasing to God, continuing the mission of Jesus.

FOR YOUR FOLDER

1. What is the Great Commission?
2. Name one thing Jesus commanded the disciples to do after his resurrection
3. How can an ordinary Christian live out the Great Commission today?

IN A GROUP

Some people think that it is fine to have religious faith as long as you keep it to yourself. Do you think Christians have the right to tell others about their faith? Give reasons for your answer, showing that you have considered more than one point of view.

FURTHER THINKING

How is the Great Commission carried out?
Find out about the work of missionaries from your local churches and parishes or using the internet.
Some examples include:

COCM Chinese Overseas Christian mission
www.cocm.org.uk

SIM Serving in Mission
www.sim.co.uk

CBM Christian Blind Mission
www.cbmuk.org.uk

Mission Africa
www.missionafrica.org.uk

OMF – Overseas Missionary Fellowship
www.omf.org.uk

Index

Acknowledgements

Author's acknowledgements

Thanks are due to a number of people who contributed to this book: Sam Smith from the Leprosy Mission, Father John, Steve Stockman, and the Red Nose Day team.

Special thanks goes to Donna Finlay (CCEA); Joan Williams (CCEA); Philip Barnes (CCEA); Sheila Johnston and Michael Spence at Colourpoint for their thorough guidance throughout the editing process; Martin, Tom and Kate for their patience. I dedicate this book to my sister and friend, Noreen Kennedy.

Picture credits

Cover image: iStockphoto

iStockphoto: 5, 7, 9 (top right), 11, 12 (both), 13 (middle), 14 (bottom two), 19, 21, 23 (both), 24 (both), 25, 26 (top right), 27 (both), 30, 31, 32, 33 (both), 35, 39, 41 (left), 42 (left), 43 (both right), 44 (right), 45 (top right), 46, 47, 48 (top right), 50, 51 (background), 52, 53, 54 (left), 55 (left), 56 (top right), 59 (both), 61, 63, 64 (both), 65 (bottom left), 66, 67

Alex Eleon: 9 (bottom right)
Masqueraid: 15 (left)
Peter Martin: 24 (Top right, background), 44 (bottom left)
Gugganij: 26 (left)
Michael Spence: 48 (bottom right), 49 (top right)
Steve Stockman: 55 (left)